To Live is to Pray

C000185072

ELIZABETH RUTH OBBARD is the novice mistress at the Carmel of Walsingham in Norfolk. She is the author of a number of books which she has also illustrated, including *A Walsingham Prayer Book*, *The History and Spirituality of Walsingham* and *See How I Love You – Meditations on the Way of the Cross with Julian of Norwich*, all published by the Canterbury Press Norwich.

Other titles in the *Rhythm of Life* series

RHYTHM *of* LIFE

SERIES EDITOR : BISHOP GRAHAM CHADWICK

TO LIVE

is to

PRAY

An introduction to Carmelite Spirituality

ELIZABETH OBBARD

ODC

CANTERBURY
PRESS
Norwich

Text and illustrations © Elizabeth Ruth Obbard ODC 1997

First published 1997 by The Canterbury Press Norwich
(a publishing imprint of Hymns Ancient & Modern Limited,
a registered charity)
St Mary's Works, St Mary's Plain,
Norwich, Norfolk, NR3 3BH

British Library Cataloging in Publication Data

A catalogue record for this book is available
from the British Library

ISBN 1-85311-182-1

*Typeset by David Gregson Associates, Beccles, Suffolk and
printed by Athenæum Press Ltd, Gateshead, Tyne & Wear*

for HELEN and PENNY
'... beginning to be servants of Love'
St Teresa

Contents

Acknowledgements

I have freely used several versions of the works quoted in order to keep the style conversational. I am indebted especially to the Allison Peers translation of the *Complete Works of St Teresa of Avila*, Sheed and Ward, 1946; to the David Lewis translation of the *Complete Works of St John of the Cross*, Longmans, 1864; to Donald Attwater's translation of *The Practice of the Presence of God*, Burns and Oates, 1926; to the Ronald Knox translation of *The Story of a Soul* (St Thérèse of Lisieux) Fontana, 1958, with a separate translation of Manuscript B by Margaret Needham ODC; and to the ICS version of the *Complete Works of Elizabeth of the Trinity* translated by Aletheia Kane ODC, ICS Publications, 1984.

Series Introduction

✖

*Wisdom is to discern the true rhythm of things:
joy is to move, to dance to that rhythm.*

These books on various traditions of Christian
spirituality are intended as introductions for
beginners on the journey of faith. They might help
us discover a truer rhythm as something of the
experience of those who follow any particular tradition resonates with our own.

Too much can be made of the distinctions between
the different expressions of Christian spirituality.
They all derive from the experience of what God has
done and is doing in us and among us. While
emphases differ, their validity is their congruence
with the good news of Jesus Christ in the scriptures. As the various instruments in an orchestra
make their special contribution to the symphony, so
we delight in the extra dimension that each tradition brings to the living out of the Christian faith.

The present wide interest in spirituality seems to
indicate that, in the midst of all the current uncer-
tainties that we meet in contemporary life, despite
its relative comfort and technological advance,
there is felt a need to reconnect with our spiritual
roots and find a deeper purpose for living.

Each volume offers an introduction to the essential elements of the particular spiritual tradition
and practical guidance for shaping our everyday
lives according to its teaching and wisdom. It is an
exploration into the way that spiritual practice can
affect our lifestyle, work, relationships, our view of
creation, patterns of prayer and worship, and
responsibilities in the wider world.

Many books, of course, have been written in all of these areas and in each tradition classic commentaries are available which can never be surpassed. The aim of this series is to meet the needs of those searching for or beginning to explore the journey inward into their inmost being and outward to relationship with people and the whole of creation.

The word 'mystic' can be mysterious and frightening, suggesting something beyond us ordinary mortals. But a mystic has been described as 'a person who has fallen in love with God'. Lovers attract us by their single-mindedness and their longing to be one with the object of their love. The six Carmelites described in this book attract us to themselves and encourage us to follow in their search for God, the great Lover. The authenticity of our love for God is proven by the quality of our relationship to people and our concern for social justice. My hope is that, pondering on the lives of these saints, readers will be helped on their own inward and outward journey and to find a truer rhythm of life.

BISHOP GRAHAM CHADWICK
Sarum College
Ascensiontide, 1997

Introduction

It was the era of the Crusades when a small group of hermits established themselves on the holy mountain of Carmel in the north of Palestine, and made it their home. They had discovered a valley – the Wadi es Siah – secluded and sheltered, with a beautiful view over the sea, near the city of Acre where the crusader ships docked. It was fertile country, with land able to provide for their simple needs. The wadi was off the main travelling routes and permeated with memories of the Old Testament figure of Elijah who, on Carmel, had challenged the prophets of Baal and vindicated the power of the God of Israel.

The conquest of Jerusalem by the crusader armies in 1091 had witnessed an upsurge of devotion to the human Christ, Jesus of Nazareth, who had lived and loved in historical Palestine, walked its paths and known its hills and rivers. His eyes had gazed on the plain of Esdraelon, bright with spring anemones, the 'lilies of the field'. His feet had passed along the streets of Jerusalem as he approached the temple precincts for prayer, and he had been nailed to the cross on the site of Calvary. At Bethlehem, the reputed cave of the nativity could be venerated. From Nazareth, the Christian pilgrim could gaze over the horizon which Jesus' own eyes had scanned, with Carmel rearing its stately peaks in the distance, the glittering blue of the sea visible beyond. In the Bible, Carmel was a mountain synonymous with fertility and beauty, lush with vegetation and vineyards.

With Palestine at least temporarily in Christian hands, people flocked to see the sites hallowed by the presence of the Son of God. Many decided to stay in the area and not return to the Europe they had left behind. They set up hermitages and retired to pray and meditate in solitude beside the River Jordan, in the Judaen desert, on the outskirts of Bethlehem, or at Nazareth, Jerusalem, Thabor and Carmel. Some were pilgrims who now ceased their wanderings, having reached the goal of their dreams; still others were erstwhile crusaders who had arrived full of high ideals and then were sickened at the violence and bloodshed, rape and looting, that accompanied fighting men wherever they went. Changing their allegiance from an earthly master to that of the Prince of Peace, they took to prayer in the country they had come to liberate.

As the Christian forces were gradually pushed back by the Saracens, hermits who had established themselves around Jerusalem and Judaea fled northwards, where Carmel and the city of Acre were still under crusader rule. They found other hermits there already and joined them. They were a motley gathering from a variety of countries – Scandinavia, ·France, England, Italy, Cyprus .... comprising former pilgrims, travellers, crusaders from many social classes and national backgrounds. They would be conscious of being allied with a long spiritual tradition of men and women who, over the centuries, had retired to the desert to live for God alone, far from the enticements of a corrupt society.

In direct contrast to the great monastic foundations, isolated hermits would sometimes combine together in small groups to give one another spiritual and material support. They would pray in the vicinity of their individual cells for most of the day and lived in poverty, cultivating a small vegetable garden, weaving baskets or mats, but having others close at hand in case of need or sickness. It was a free-flowing life. Hermits focussed primarily on closeness to Christ, continual prayer in solitude and the recitation of the psalter as they went about their simple daily tasks.

The group of hermits on Carmel, because of their location, looked to Elijah as their special patron and archetype. Indeed, Elijah had long been invoked as the forerunner of those who chose a monastic or solitary life, linked as he was with John the Baptist – desert-dweller and forerunner of the Lord. As it was the end of the twelfth and beginning of the thirteenth century when the group we are speaking of settled on Carmel, Mary too had a primary place in their devotion. She was then being invoked throughout Christendom as mother, queen and beloved companion, the model of the ideal woman, who infused feudal Europe with a new sense of chivalry and an appreciation of all that was feminine.

Sometime between 1209 and 1214, the hermits of Carmel asked the Patriarch of Jerusalem, Albert of Avogadro (then resident at Acre), to provide them with a basic Rule that would guide them in their solitary way of life and could be passed on as a pattern to those who would come after. Albert obliged in the form of a letter, exhorting the hermits to persevere in prayer, 'meditating day and night on the law of the Lord' in the solitude of their cells. They were to elect a prior and promise him obedience. There was to be a chapel built for daily Mass and there was to be a weekly meeting. The whole of Albert's Rule is a tissue of scriptural texts, skilfully woven to provide a pattern of life suitable for those dedicated to the Lord in a radical way. It is in the Rule of St Albert, together with the tradition of the desert fathers and mothers, that we find the roots of Carmelite spirituality. It is simple, direct and biblically based, a life of 'allegiance to Christ' closely tied to the Holy Land and the mountain of Carmel. With the Carmelites there is no one dominant founder as is the case with the Benedictines, Franciscans, Dominicans and Jesuits; instead, there is only a group. But in this lies Carmel's strength. There is a breadth and depth in Carmelite spirituality which makes it able to accommodate many approaches and many types of people. Carmel is for all, not just for an élite.

As the numbers on Carmel increased, so the position of the Europeans – identified with an army of occupation – became ever more precarious. Some of the hermits decided to leave Palestine and return to their countries of origin. One of the earliest groups came to England in 1240 and gradually established themselves, the main foundations being at Aylesford in Kent and Hulne in Northumberland. But a way of life designed for a warm climate could not long survive in Europe without adaptation.

One option would have been to embrace a formalized monastic life style, the alternative was to join the new mendicant movement established by St Francis and St Dominic. The brothers chose the latter, but according to their own heritage and tradition; for underneath, the spirit of Carmel remained the same: solitude, continual prayer, closeness to ordinary people, and the inspiration of the great archetypes – Mary and Elijah.

Carmel as 'land', Carmel as spirituality, the brothers discovered, was not tied only to a certain place and an unchanging interpretation, it was also broad enough to be adapted and modified so as to meet the needs of new situations. Since those first days on the holy mountain, friars, priests, contemplative nuns, apostolic sisters and brothers, lay men and women, have all found ways to share in Carmel's heritage.

There are certainly great Carmelite saints whose names are known to all – Teresa of Avila, John of the Cross, Thérèse of Lisieux. But there are also countless anonymous people (like the first hermits) who have embodied the same spirit of prayer, who have found inspiration in Mary and Elijah, and have been content to contribute in hidden ways to the Church's holiness in a spirit of simplicity and joy.

Many seem to think that Carmelite life is austere and forbidding, that it demands more than the average person can give. It is true that all gospel spirituality, if it is authentic, asks for a totally committed following of Christ. But Jesus himself took people where they were, not where others thought they should be, and invited them to participate in accepting and spreading the good news of the kingdom. At the Last Supper he promised that his presence would remain, through the gift of the Spirit, in all who loved him and had the courage to love others; and that such lives would bear fruit because they were united to his own. He offered this as an ideal for all, though it would obviously take different forms in different people. In the same way, living by the spirituality of Carmel takes many different outward forms, but basically it is unified by a spirit of prayer and closeness to Christ that has deep roots and a long tradition. Each one will put his or her own unique stamp on their understanding of the Carmelite path and the Carmelite heritage.

In this book, Carmelite spirituality will be seen and savoured through six different interpreters who have left their mark on the Order: Simon of England, Brother Lawrence, Teresa of Avila, John of the Cross, Thérèse of Lisieux and Elizabeth of the Trinity. Each one can teach us something of what it means to live and pray within the Carmelite family. For this reason I have allowed each one to speak for him or her self, sharing with the reader what Carmel has meant to them in their own lives and how they see it contributing to the lives of those who look to them as leaders and teachers. They are models of the journey of prayer, which is ultimately the journey we must all make to find and savour God and the intimacy he offers.

Chapter 1

The Roots of a Tradition – St Simon of England

Simon of England, also called St Simon Stock, is a man of whom very little is known; presumably, however, he was a native of Kent who joined the hermit brothers on Mount Carmel sometime in the early days of the Rule. Returning later to England, he was instrumental in carrying out the changes needed for the Order to adapt itself to a new form of religious life in Europe, while still retaining its essential eremitical orientation. Simon was known for his personal devotion to Mary. He died at Bordeaux sometime towards the end of the thirteenth century.

As Simon of England is such a shadowy figure, lost in the mists of legend, he can be used to personify the first generations of Carmelites. He speaks for them all as he sits in the corner of his bare cell, his face partially hidden by the folds of the hood covering his head. He is old and he wraps his striped mantle around him to stave off the chill

1

wind that blows through the shutters. Behind him, on a small, rough pillar of wood, stands a rudely carved image of the Virgin and Child with a few wild flowers before it in a clay bowl.

Simon Speaks

I am an old man now and I have travelled a lot; not really by choice, but that's how things have turned out for me. I was born here in Kent, not far from Aylesford, which is my home base at present. My father was a freedman, quite well off, but gruff and surly. My mother died when I was very young so I grew up relying mainly on my own resources. I never seemed to be like the other boys on the manor; I was continually drawn to pray in the church, and I was aware of God's presence in the woods and fields about me and under the silent stars glittering above at night.

My father thought I might have a vocation to the monastic life, so I travelled to Canterbury and talked to some of the monks there. They follow the Rule of St Benedict and sing the Offices in a magnificent cathedral. They illuminate manuscripts too and have a veritable city-enclave of crafts and charitable works. It was all too grand for me, I wanted a simpler life, closer to the soil, closer to people and, as I thought, closer to the life of Jesus himself, who was a poor man.

When I was twenty-two, I decided to be a hermit. I received a plain tunic to signify my dedication and built myself a hut in the forest. There I could pray and think, there I could be alone with God as I wanted. I also kept the small bridge over the river Medway in good repair, showed travellers where the stream could be forded, and kept 'open hut' for anyone who happened to be passing. We'd share a meal of vegetables from my garden, and milk and cheese from the goat. I became proficient with herbs and would soon brew up a healing potion if a passing pilgrim or merchant suffered from bruises and cuts or shivered with fever.

When I heard that a ship was leaving from London, taking men and women to Palestine – a land opened up for the Christians by crusaders – I decided to join them. We were a motley band setting out: housewives, priests, converted criminals doing penance for their crimes, traders. It was a long and dangerous journey and a number died en route.

At last we disembarked at Acre. I detached myself from the others and made off to visit the places which Jesus had known and loved. It seemed like a dream come true for me, praying at Bethlehem, Nazareth and Calvary. As the weeks merged into months I knew I could never return to England. The Holy Land was now *my* land. I discovered that there was a company of hermits living on Mount Carmel and went to visit them. There were already one or two Englishmen in the group, and when I passed along the gorge and into the valley where they had their hermitages I knew that I was 'home'.

The Rule was still new and things were pretty unstructured. It was the simple kind of hermit life I had been living by myself in Kent, but now I had the support of a community – friends around me, all sharing the same ideal. We took it in turn to prepare meals and deliver the food to the others in their cells. We met together for daily Mass and a weekly discussion. Our little chapel dedicated to Mary soon attracted pilgrims who came to pray on the mountain made holy by the prophet Elijah.

I was all set to end my days in peace in the land of

Christ's birth, when I was suddenly asked if I would join a group of brothers who were setting sail for England with Sir Richard de Grey, a crusader. The situation in Palestine was becoming more unstable and it had been decided that the brothers should gradually seek security in Europe to guarantee the future of our manner of life. We had talked about this, of course, but somehow I had never expected to be personally involved. I was well past middle age and it was as if I was having to tear my heart out, detach myself from the place which had become dear and familiar, and put down roots in a new soil. Also I had friends in the wadi who I would be leaving behind (it's surprising how one *does* make special friends even in the solitary life) and the surroundings of Carmel were congenial to my temperament which likes stability and beauty. It was a terrible wrench, but I did it.

We sailed back to England by way of the Thames, whose grey waters had witnessed my departure so many years ago. We were presented to King Henry at Westminster, then we divided up and went our separate ways. Being from Kent, I was with those who came to Aylesford where Sir Richard had given us lands and a house. We took possession on Christmas Day 1240, feeling cold, weary and home-sick for the warm climate we had left behind. It was only later that it occurred to me that Bethlehem must have seemed like that to Mary when she gave birth to the Lord in a draughty stable far from her own familiar dwelling at Nazareth.

Time swiftly proved that we couldn't live in England as we had done in the East. The climate was different for a start. We needed more nourishing food and better houses. We needed to provide for young men who might join us and we needed to earn our living. By 1247 we had settled on changes which would enable us to adapt more easily to our new environment. We would remain praying communities, close to ordinary people, but we would also provide services like preaching which would ensure an income. Some of the brothers weren't happy about this. It's always easier to cling to old ways and not rise to the challenge, so my life now is mostly spent in travelling around, explaining why things have to be as they are now and why we can't remain in an idyllic past (which, I have to admit, was not nearly so idyllic as some try to make out). Personally, although outward observances have changed somewhat, we're more together in community for one thing; I find a unifying thread running through my life, linking together my solitary hermit existence, my years on Carmel and my life now as a man on the move, yet drawing strength from prayer. There are three things at the basis of Carmelite spirituality as I and my hermit brothers understand it. Firstly, allegiance to Christ (which finds expression in love for Mary, his mother); secondly, the figure of Elijah; and lastly, the call of the desert. I'll explain each one in more detail.

Love for Mary

Mary has always had a special place in the life of Carmelites. We were the first Order to call ourselves after her, becoming the 'Brothers of St Mary of Mount Carmel'. Our first chapel in the Wadi es Siah was dedicated to her. She is the woman who, as 'lady of the place', seems to permeate the land of Carmel with her presence.

In the Bible, the mountain of Carmel was used as an image of loveliness and fertility.[1] When I was there the flowers, the vines, the wooded slopes, all recalled the beauty of the mother of God. Sometimes I would climb to the top of the mountain and gaze over the sparkling Mediterranean Sea. It was here that Elijah had bowed himself to the ground and prayed for rain after his contest with the prophets of Baal. Here he had seen a distant cloud rising as if from the blue waters, heralding rain for the drought-parched earth.[2] Christian tradition has long seen in this cloud an image of Mary. As clouds carry rain, so she, the Godbearer, brought the one whose coming heralded life and refreshment for us poor humans, so dry and needy without salvation. I would think of all this as I laid before Mary my own needs and the cries and prayers of the whole suffering world. After all, the hermit's cell is supposed to be enclosed only on three sides, since the fourth side must be open to accept and intercede for all humanity, loving and caring for it with all the tenderness of a mother.

We hermits of Carmel have always known Mary not only as mother but also as sister, companion and friend. Looking at her in Scripture we can see that the kind of holiness she embodies is available to all. It is a holiness of radical openness to the Lord, as at the Annunciation when she listens to the angel's message and responds with her *Fiat* – 'be it done to me according to your word'. Then there is her joy at the Visitation when she carries the unborn Christ to Elizabeth and sings her Magnificat. She brings him to birth and offers him to the Father at the Presentation in the Temple. She is there too with Jesus, standing at the foot of the cross as he dies. And between the beginning and end of his life she gives him space to be himself and to fulfil his mission while she ponders everything in her heart[3] – the attitude of a true contemplative.

Our Rule bids us to pray unceasingly. Mary is our model in this too. She was an ordinary Jewish wife and mother with a household to manage. She did not isolate herself from her neighbours and village community. She had to find matter for prayer in everything; in daily life as well as in times of solitude. Hers is the way of faith, not sight. 'Blessed is she who believed,' says Elizabeth at the Visitation.[4]

Looking at Mary I find one in whom I can confide, one who brings me to Jesus, one who accompanies me as I try to respond to God in the changing circumstances of my life. Mary is the one who enables me to be present, silently and humbly, with those who suffer, with those who wait, with those who are confused. As I grew up without a mother myself, I find in her one who understands so well my own human and emotional needs, while encouraging me to care for others in my turn: first of all my brothers in community, each one with their own weaknesses, foibles and wounds, and then everyone who touches my life in one way or another. Carmel, as an image of Mary, is a beautiful mountain inciting one to prayer and praise. But I've discovered that Mary travels with me even when I'm not in that holy land I love so well. Mary is *here*. She is 'lady of the place' in England too, and indeed wherever she is given space in anyone's life or heart.

Mary of Carmel is queen of the contemplative life because she teaches us pre-eminently to walk the path of faith which, as our Rule says, must be our shield on all occasions.

> She teaches us how to listen, how to explore, how to accept, to make sacrifices. She teaches us how to meditate, to wait, to examine. She teaches us self-possession and calm, absolute assurance in judge-

ment and action. She teaches us, in short, the fulness of prayer and communion with God. And all these things, though we see them in Mary uniquely realized by that one soul who was full of grace and completely under the sway of the Holy Spirit, are yet all forms of faith, and therefore close to us and available not only for our admiration but for our imitation.[5]

Mary teaches me too how all things work together for good for those who love God.[6] They did for her and I am confident that this will prove true for me as well.

Mary has been my companion since boyhood, the 'lady' of my choice, just as the crusading knights chose their lady. She has walked with me all along the way. To her I have dedicated my life as a Carmelite and in this Order I know she will always be specially honoured. Mary is our model in her surrender to the will of God, in her constant fidelity. Even the clothes I wear, my religious habit, is a reminder of how she clothed Jesus at his birth and again wove for him the seamless garment which the soldiers gambled for at his crucifixion. Being clothed like this is an expression of wanting to be clothed by her in the garments of true Christlikeness: in compassion, kindness, lowliness, meekness, patience, in mutual forebearance and forgiveness, binding all together with the cloak of love.[7]

As I grow older, and indeed I am now very old, I feel Mary calling me to enter into the mystery of death with Jesus so that I will ultimately know the joy of resurrection, just as Mary experienced her Assumption, body and soul, into the presence of God. Mary's Assumption is the great feast of this house at Aylesford and I love to hymn her with these words on behalf of myself and the whole Order:

> Flower of Carmel, blossoming bearing one,
> Light of heaven, mother of God's dear Son,
> Vine and Virgin.
>
> Gentle parent, pure beyond human love,
> Bless your children, star shining far above
> This world's ocean.

The Prophet Elijah

It is only natural that the prophet Elijah gave us hermits inspiration, living as we did on the mountain he had made holy by his presence; and I have meditated continually on all the Bible tells us about him.

Elijah was first and foremost a man of prayer, but also a man of action and courage. He was a man of solitude but also a man of the people. In the Book of Kings he seems to come from nowhere, reliant on God, departing to dwell near the brook, Cherith, at God's command.[8] I've tried to do what that signifies in my own life: live in charity, the spirit of love, drink from the waters of prayer, and depend on providence as Elijah depended on the ravens to bring him food.

The best known story of Elijah is, of course, the incident where he encounters God on Mount Horeb after he has won his victory over the prophets of Baal on Carmel.[9] Weary and disillusioned, he journeys into the desert and rests in a cave on the very mountain where Moses had encountered the Lord en route to the Promised Land. 'What are you doing here Elijah?' comes the Lord's voice. 'I have been very zealous for the Lord the God of Hosts,' he replies, in words which have become Carmel's motto. He proceeds to detail his reasons for depression, enumerating the sins of Israel and his loneliness as sole fighter for the right, whose very life is now sought. 'Go forth,' says the Lord, 'and stand in my presence.' So Elijah watches for the Lord to manifest himself. Earthquake, fire and wind follow one another in quick succession, but the Lord is not to be found in these. At last a still, small voice is heard, the whisper of a gentle breeze, and then Elijah knows this is the moment. Wrapping his face in his mantle, he goes to stand at the cave's mouth and to listen to the Lord's directions for future action.

Prayer is about listening to that still small voice in silence, recognizing it and responding, so that action does not spring from one's own initiative but from God's word. Elijah, in listening, was not commanded to retire further into the wilderness but to go back to the milieu he had left and anoint a new king and a prophetic successor in Elisha. Often we hear things in prayer that we would rather not hear. This is the test. Does God matter more, or have we our own plans all mapped out anyway and only want the Lord's approval?

It seems that Elijah had a group of followers called 'sons of the prophet' and that, at the end of his life, he let his mantle fall from the fiery chariot on to Elisha, that Elisha might receive in his turn a double share of Elijah's spirit.[10] We Carmelites may not be able to claim literal descent in an unbroken line from those earliest days of prophetic witness, but we do see ourselves as spiritually bonded to Elijah, Elisha and those who followed them. In this, we are in line with the whole of religious life.

10

[Elijah] lived in God's presence and contemplated his passing by in silence; he interceded for the people and boldly announced God's will; he defended God's sovereignty and came to the defence of the poor against the powerful of the world (cf. 1 Kings 18–19). In the history of the Church, alongside other Christians, there have been men and women consecrated to God who, through a special gift of the Holy Spirit, have carried out a genuinely prophetic ministry, speaking in the name of God to all, even to the pastors of the Church. True prophecy is born of God, from friendship with him, from attentive listening to his word in the different circumstances of history. Prophets feel in their hearts a burning desire for the holiness of God and, having heard his word in the dialogue of prayer, they proclaim that word with their lives, with their lips and with their actions, becoming people who speak for God against evil and sin. Prophetic witness requires the constant and passionate search for God's will, for self-giving, for unfailing communion in the Church, for the practice of spiritual discernment and love for the truth. It is also expressed through the denunciation of all that is contrary to the divine will and through the exploration of new ways to apply the Gospel in history, in expectation of the coming of the kingdom of God.[11]

A Carmelite has to have courage to act in the spirit of Elijah as well as possessing a silent heart like Mary. There has to be a combination of both masculine and feminine elements to make the whole person.

Elijah also highlights our indebtedness to the Old Testament, gives our lives a sense of continuity with the past just as Mary does.

Often on Mount Carmel I would ponder the Elijah stories, walking the mountain slopes that he had known, standing in the place of sacrifice where he had confronted the priests of Baal. I seemed to hear

11

him challenging me not to go limping with two different opinions, not to dither and be indecisive, not to be a person of compromise but to choose and re-choose the Lord wholeheartedly at every juncture of my life.[12]

That has become even more of a reality since I came back to England and was plunged into a life so different from the solitude I had cherished. I've discovered by experience that being available to God isn't about fulfilling one's own ambitions and dreams, but God's – going where *God* wants one to go which isn't necessarily where one would choose.

It's my hope that, as Elijah witnessed the Transfiguration of Jesus so I, too, will one day see the Lord in glory and he will become the great reality of my life. Anything less just isn't worthwhile.

Solitude and Continual Prayer

'Each one of you is to stay in his own cell, pondering the Lord's law day and night unless attending to some other duty,' our Rule states.

We stand in a long tradition of desert fathers and mothers, and our Rule lays great stress on solitude as an aid to prayer. In most other monasteries, monks sleep in common dormitories and work in general workrooms and scriptoria in great monastic buildings. We, on the contrary, have chosen the option open to the hermits of old by preserving individual cells and working alone as far as possible. True we are mendicants, friars like the Franciscans and Dominicans. We can live in small communities in towns and be close to the poor by our more ordinary life style; but even so, we never forget our desert roots. That's a heritage we cherish.

Jesus advised his disciples to pray in secret and as Brothers of Carmel we have preserved this facet of eremitical life, even though our cells are in a certain proximity to one another and we have never been in such isolation that we cut off all encounters with the people living around us.[13]

Looking to Jesus as our model of prayer we keep in mind his own practice of prayer at night, when he would retire from the crowds and go away alone to commune with his Father. *Was it not our Lord and Saviour who led us into the desert as a mark of his favour, so that he might speak to our hearts with special intimacy? To a mountain solitude did our Saviour ascend alone to pray; though we read that he came down from the mountain when he would preach to the people and manifest his works.*[14]

The first desert fathers and mothers were eminently practical people, compassionate, not hampered by numerous rules, ready to respond to needs as Elijah responded to the widow of Zarephath.[15] We don't want our solitude to be selfish and self-protective. One of the stories of the first desert fathers tells of how a brother asked an old man, 'There are two brothers. One of them stays in his cell quietly while fasting for six days at a time and imposing on himself a good deal of discipline, and the other serves the sick. Which of them is more acceptable to God?' The old man replied, 'Even if the brother who fasts six days were to hang himself by the nose he could not equal the one who serves the sick.'[16] A pure and compassionate heart knows when to pray and when to act as circumstances arise. Carmel is about an inner attitude: the attitude of freedom, of poverty, of availability, without too many preconceived notions of what that entails.

13

This inner attitude has enabled me to preserve my solitude and spirit of prayer through all of my life's changes. I hope I am now a person rooted in God and carry my 'cell' wherever I go.

For Reflection

1. Can you find some examples in your own life of how St Paul's words to the Romans – that 'by turning everything to their good God co-operates with those who love him' (Romans 8:28) – can be true for you? Write down events and experiences you have lived through and look for the thread of God's guidance in them. Write your own canticle of gratitude, your personal *Magnificat* including, if you can, even what has been painful and disorienting.

2. Meditate on these words from the Carmelite hymn *Flos Carmeli*, asking Mary to be with you as you pray them and give you ever deeper insight into their meaning.

   Holy Lady, Carmel's great friend and queen,
   Feast your people from your own bliss, the unseen grace,
   God's goodness.

3. How can Mary be friend, mother and companion in your own life? Find an icon or picture that speaks to you and display it somewhere where it can remind you of her attentive pondering on the word of God.

4. Re-read the story in the Book of Kings where Elijah encounters God in the whisper of a gentle breeze (1 Kings 19:4–13). Make a resolution to attend to even the slightest whisper of God as he

speaks to you through the events of your own life.

5. If you do not already have one, ask a priest to bless a Carmelite scapular (the 'apron' that symbolizes the yoke of Christ) for you and wear it as a reminder that you are linked spiritually to the Order of Carmel, and most especially to Mary as its queen and patron. Pray that you may be used as an instrument of Christ's presence to all you meet.

6. How can you find ways to nourish the spirit of prayer and solitude that is proper to Carmel? Is there some place in your home where you can make a corner of solitude to retire to from time to time? Are there moments, even in a busy day, when you can retire to the cell of your heart and offer a prayer to re-orient you Godwards? Resolve on some specific moments when you will do just this.

NOTES
1 Cf. Isaiah 35:2; Song of Songs 7:5
2 1 Kings 18:41–46
3 Luke 2:19, 51
4 Luke 1:45
5 From an address by Pope Paul VI (Carmelite Breviary for 16 July)
6 Romans 8:28
7 Colossians 3:12–14
8 1 Kings 17:3
9 1 Kings 19:4–18
10 2 Kings 2:9–14
11 *Vita Consecrata*, Apostolic Exhortation of John Paul II on the Religious Life, CTS, 1996, pp. 155–6
12 1 Kings 18:21
13 Matthew 6:6
14 *The Flaming Arrow*, Nicholas of Narbonne, a contemporary of St Simon of England, trans. M. Edwards, Teresian Press, 1985 p. 29

15 1 Kings 17:8–24
16 *Desert Wisdom, Sayings of the Desert Fathers*, Yushi Nomura, Doubleday, 1984, p. 66

Chapter 2

Starting Out on the Way of Prayer – St Teresa of Avila

Teresa of Avila (1515–82) is arguably the most illustrious member of the Carmelite Order. Born into a well-to-do Spanish family with Jewish *conversos* ancestry, she entered the Carmelite convent of the Incarnation in her native city at the age of twenty-one. There she lived a good, but not particularly outstanding, life as a nun until her definitive conversion in middle age.

From then onwards Teresa advanced rapidly along the mystical path and was inspired to found houses for nuns who would live by the Rule of St Albert without compromise or mitigation. However, she took into account the women of her day and devised a balanced and practical life style suited to their needs. She was also instrumental in founding reformed houses of friars.

17

Teresa was a consummate teacher who spent her remaining years helping people of all sorts towards a deeper and more authentic manner of prayer based on close observation of her own and others' life and experience. She was a born organizer, practical, witty, attractive, gifted for friendship: an outstanding woman by any measure. It was she who gave form to the life of the Discalced nuns who look to her as their mother and foundress. Her books are recognized classics of spirituality and, together with her nuns, are ways in which she continues to live on today.

Teresa spent many hours travelling the roads of Spain extending her Reform, and she speaks to us now with the same directness that is the mark of all her writing. We meet her seated in a bullock cart, bouncing along a rough road on her way to view a site for another possible convent. All contemporary descriptions of Teresa speak of her as a fine-looking woman, inclined to plumpness, with sparkling black eyes and expressive white hands, always in motion. There is a bigness about her presence which invites confidence – physically big as she is, she has a heart and wit to match.

Teresa Speaks

I'm convinced, really convinced, that the greatest gift anyone can give to Christ and his Church is to be a person of prayer, because by prayer we enter into a relationship with God and only God can make us holy. My whole life so far has been given to helping people to pray, that includes my own sisters, who often enter one of my convents expecting to hear all about visions and revelations. I don't buy into all that nonsense! Those things are only 'sweets' and not the real article at all. God works differently with different people and temperaments and my experience has shown me that no one will get anywhere unless they realize that prayer is about a whole Godward way of life, not just about hours of silence and solitude and spiritual things like sermons and holy books.

When the sisters asked me to write a book for them, specifically for beginners in prayer, I gave them the *Way of Perfection*. They were very surprised to find that the first chapters were all about how to live well and the kind of dispositions needed if we are to come close to God. The motto of Carmel is Elijah's cry: 'With zeal I have been zealous for the Lord God of Hosts.' I've made that my motto too and applied it specifically to the life of prayer which is Carmel's special mission in the Church. The Church needs zealous pray-ers, and *all of us who wear the holy habit of Carmel* (and indeed all who live by Carmel's spirituality) *are called to prayer and contemplation, because we are descended from the first hermits who sought God in solitude and retirement.*[1]

There are a number of misconceptions about what a life of prayer entails and it's no good talking about high-flown words like 'contemplation' without first saying something about what those who walk this path (entering into the process of prayer would be another way of putting it) must lay as foundations. Good actions are absolutely necessary or we would be deceiving ourselves. *Love for others, detachment and true humility*[2] have to be growing all the time and interacting with our prayer if it is to be genuine.

When founding my convents I devised a balanced manner of life that would incorporate plenty of opportunities for developing these three things.

Close community living in a family-like environment, regular, set times for prayer and solitude, times of recreation – all are ideal for experiencing human weakness, one's own and others', at close quarters, because we keep strict enclosure and can't escape through outward distractions.

However, nobody is barred from deep prayer. Everyone's life affords occasions for practising virtue. Life is life wherever it is lived. We all have more or less the same struggles, the same failings and the same path to tread before we come to the goal: union with God.

Love of Others

The Lord himself said that what we do to others we do to him[3] and he wanted the mark of his disciples to be that of mutual love.[4] I have seen that to concentrate on this is a sure way of following Christ and is, indeed, essential. *Our Lord asks only two things of us: love of God and love of our neighbour. If we attain these virtues in their perfection we are doing the Lord's will and will be united to him as he promised. Now, the only sure sign that we are keeping these two commandments is that we are in fact loving our neighbour. For we cannot be sure that we are loving God, even though we may have good reasons for believing that we are; but we can know quite well whether or not we are loving others.*[5] You can be certain that the more you advance in love of neighbour, God will reward you in a thousand ways by increasing the love you bear to him. Both are intertwined at the root. It's no good making fine plans in prayer about how you will love others if you don't actually do so when the opportunity arises. That reveals your prayer as airy daydreaming without substance.

20

When I see people trying hard to discover what kind of prayer they are experiencing, all wrapped up in their devotions and afraid to move in case they lose their recollection, I realize how little they understand.[6] They think everything consists in tender emotions and tears. Good gracious no! They have got it all wrong! Look outwards, not inwards! Is somebody sick? Help them, take their pain on yourself, be sympathetic. If someone is hungry, go without food yourself to ensure that they can eat. If you hear someone being praised, rejoice in their good fortune instead of sulking. If you can relieve another of a trial, do so. Think of the love which Jesus had in bearing his cross and you'll find strength to go out of yourself and your own self-centred little world. Ask the Lord to grant you perfect love of neighbour and leave the rest to him. You won't lose anything by it.

As for faults – *let's learn to look at our own short-comings and leave other people's alone. Those who are trying to live pious lives are much too prone to be shocked by everything; whereas we can often learn important lessons from the very people who shock us.*[7] Outward behaviour isn't a priority, inward motivation is what counts, and we can't judge anyone else's inner motives – that's God's business. And don't forget – others are putting up with *our* faults, including many *we* are blissfully unaware of!

Let us strive then always to look at the virtues and good qualities we see in people around us and keep our own sins before our eyes. Don't let us notice the speck in our neighbour's eye when there is a beam in our own.[8] *This is a course of action which, though we may not become perfect in it at once, will help us acquire one great virtue – namely, to consider others better than ourselves.*[9] Genuine

21

love on our part is shown by how willingly we put ourselves out on account of others. This is a much truer love than using all kinds of affectionate expressions, although tenderness has its place at the proper time.

If we are sincere in our relationships – open, loving, alert to the good – we will make friends who support us in our search for God, and friends have been a great boon in my own life. Also, by loving rightly, we discover the core of the other person which is always lovable. We aren't seduced by ephemeral qualities like youth, charm or pleasant manners. We love the real person, not the façade.

I have a gift for friendship. I enjoy company; but I've learned how to keep all this in right order, loving all, excluding no one, letting my heart be stretched wide. The more room you make for others, the more room there is for God to come in.

Detachment and Humility

True humility and detachment always go together[10] as I see it. What do I mean by that? I think humility and detachment give us the ability to stand back and see life in its proper perspective – the perspective that gives us the possibility of acknowledging that God is far more important than our own tiny minds and miniscule universe. *We shall never succeed in knowing ourselves unless we seek to know God. Let us consider his greatness and our smallness, his purity and our impurity. Let us contrast the humility of Jesus with ours and we shall see indeed how far we are from being humble.*[11] There's a knack in always looking at Christ and not comparing ourselves with the yardstick by which we measure other people's behaviour against our own.

Once when I was wondering why our Lord so loves humility it struck me all of a sudden, without my having previously thought of it, that the reason is because God is truth itself, and to be humble is to walk in truth. It is absolutely true to say that we are nothing in ourselves, and anyone who fails to understand this is walking in falsehood.[12] Not that that thought should make us downcast. On the contrary, it should fill us with joy and gratitude for all God has given us and make us long to be more like him. True humility fosters courage and joy, not depression and self-regard.

Once we get to know and love God better we won't be so attached to such miserable possessions as our good name: *honra* (honour) we call it in Spain. My goodness, for some people, fear of 'losing face' hangs around their necks like a heavy chain. 'How can you believe, you who seek glory from one another and do not seek the glory that comes from the only God?' says Jesus.[13] Even – and, God help me, especially – in Church circles, all this chasing after titles, quarrelling about who goes first in parish processions, whether one has been addressed with sufficient respect. It makes me want to laugh, or rather, to cry, when I see people making such a fuss over their 'honour', as if their honour and God's were synonymous!

If anyone wants to make spiritual progress and finds themselves becoming punctilious about their reputation, let them believe me and put this attachment right behind them. Let them pray earnestly to God and make every effort to free themselves from this great weight which strangles and enslaves even the best of them. *I see holy people doing such wonderful things that everyone is astonished at them. God bless me! How is it that such souls are*

23

still on earth? How come they are not at the summit of perfection! Why, simply because they are pernickety about their reputation.[14] This horrid caterpillar, if allowed to flourish, will nibble away at the whole personality, leaving it warped and worm-eaten. Jesus, misunderstood and showered with insults, told us that a tree is known by its fruits.[15] Our fruits will be totally inedible and sour unless we strive to conquer ourselves on this point of sensitivity to honour. Not to mention that, even on the purely human level, the very act of desiring honour and currying favour to get it, robs us of the very thing we seek and makes us look ridiculous: *there is no poison in the world that is so fatal to perfection.*[16]

Be free, not bound. That's the way to happiness – as I know from painful experience.

Resolution
Now a bit about prayer. Sorry for the long digression but it's important not to neglect the indispensible groundwork or we are building on sand.

There's nothing I want to stress more for those setting out on the road of prayer than beginning with a firm resolution to persevere to the end – union with God. Regular time set aside for God is therefore of paramount importance. Better to spend twenty minutes regularly morning and evening come what may, than resolve on two hours a day, keep it up for a week or so when you are full of enthusiasm, then decide the whole procedure is too taxing and stop it completely, until another bout of piety takes hold of you.

Time given to God is what matters. *How* you spend it depends on yourself. There are no set rules, just do whatever helps you to love most. *I have always been fond of the words of the Gospels and have found more recollection in them than in the most carefully planned books.*[17] That doesn't mean I haven't found other books useful. In fact, *I spent twenty years needing a book at hand to help me during prayer time.*[18] Prayer is about being with Jesus, loving him, coming close to him. How we pass the time with him, what we say, isn't the main point. Time and attention given to the best of our ability are paramount.

So, *since we have resolved to give the Lord some of our time, which is indeed little compared with the amount of time we spend on ourselves and other people, let us give it freely with minds unoccupied by other things and entirely resolve not to take it back whatever we may suffer in the way of trials or dryness.*[19] Of course, we shouldn't be scrupulous or lose heart if we are sick or extra busy for a few days. The Lord isn't sitting with a watch in hand to count the minutes. It's the basic intention that is important.

If we set out resolutely as I've described we aren't so prone to the temptation to give up and we fight more courageously. Do not be afraid that the Lord who invites you to drink of living water will allow you to die of thirst. You will experience the fulfilment of his promises if you do the best you can. *Oh, how often I remember the living water the Lord spoke of to the woman of Samaria.*[20] *I am so fond of that Gospel; I have loved it since I was a child – though I did not understand it then as I do now – and I used often to beseech the Lord to give me that water. I had a picture of the Lord at the well which hung where I could see it always, and it bore the inscription 'Domine, da mihi aquam'* (Lord, give me this water).[21]

25

Such a simple thing as taking trouble with vocal prayer is a good beginning and builds up a habit that will stand anyone in good stead. Prayers said well, with attention and recollection, can lead us to the heights of contemplation.

I'll give you an example of a period spent in prayer using the Our Father. As these are Jesus' own words in which he taught us to pray we can't possibly go wrong if we stay with them.[22]

Meditating on the Lord's Prayer[23]

Preliminary
Make the sign of the cross and place yourself before God as one who is a sinner. Then, as you are alone, look for a companion – and who could be better than the very Lord who taught you the prayer you are about to say. Imagine him beside you and notice how humbly and lovingly he is teaching you. If you ask him to stay with you during prayer he will never refuse your request. It is not necessary to think about him; just *look* at him as he longs for you to do, since he is always looking at you. Keep at the side of this good Master and be most firmly resolved to learn what he is teaching you through the very words that fell from his divine lips.

Our Father
Son of God and Lord of my heart, you give so much with these first words.

How wonderful it is that you make yourself the brother of those who pray, giving us all there is to be given in making us children of the one Father, who is your Father also. Since he is truly our Father he must bear with us however great our offences. Whenever we return to him he must pardon us as he pardoned the prodigal son.

26

He must comfort us in our trials. He must sustain us as such a Father is bound to do, for he is far better than even the best of earthly parents. Everything has its perfection in him. He cherishes us, nurtures us, and ultimately makes us participants in your own divine life, Jesus, and co-heirs with you.

Behold, Lord, the love you have for us. In all humility you have taken on our nature, clothed yourself in our humanity. You are one with the Father. May you be ever blessed. Teach us, Jesus, who the Father really is, the Father you so love and honour. And may you teach us how to love and honour others rather than seeking our own advantage and boasting of our family connections. In you we are all one.

Who art in heaven
Lord, wherever you are, there is heaven.

However quietly we speak you are so near you will hear us. We do not need many words to go in search of you; we have only to find a place where we can be alone and remember your presence within us.

You are such a kind guest that we can talk to you as humbly and straightforwardly as we would to an earthly friend, asking you for whatever we want, telling you our concerns, begging your help, and all the while realizing that we are unworthy to be called your children.

Let me not be weighed down by a wrong kind of humility that is bashful or ashamed in your presence. I know that you want me to be familiar with you; to listen to you as well as talk to you. Speak to my heart and tell me all you wish.

I believe that you dwell in the heaven of my soul. Let me stay there with you, gathering myself together in your presence. Let me make the effort to remain with you so that your love has the time it needs to kindle a fire in my soul.

You have made your dwelling place within me. May I never leave you alone but give myself to you freely and completely, allowing you to do with me whatever you desire.

Hallowed be thy name, thy kingdom come
Lord Jesus, for you it was enough to ask the Father in Gesthemane that you might be resigned to his will even while you told him of your fear and your desire to have the cup of suffering pass by. But you know well that we are not as resigned as you.

We need to be taught to ask for particular things: that the Father's name be made holy, that his kingdom may come.

Lord, give me light to see, that I may want what is worth wanting and recognize it when it is given. Even here on earth we are invited to love you, Lord, with the same love as that with which the blessed love you in heaven. I ask for this gift, for it *is* a gift, not something I could earn or acquire for myself merely by my own efforts.

When Simeon came to the temple and saw the tiny infant brought in by his parents, there was nothing visible except one child among many, the son of poor people, unimportant and unrecognized. Yet you revealed who you really were to this old man. He saw beneath the surface of things to their true reality. So may I recognize your presence, find heaven all about me, praise you with my whole being.

Feed me as a mother feeds her infant at the breast. Feed me with yourself. May I want only to remain with you in silence and peace.

When you begin to give me the kingdom may I respond with all my heart, praising and glorifying your name for your mercy, responding ever more fully.

May I remain at peace with you, drawing life from your presence and from the love of your heart.

Your will be done on earth as it is in heaven

Lord, if it were not for your own example this would seem to be an impossible request. But now that my poor earth has become heaven I know that you will give me the necessary strength. Indeed, as your Father's will must be done whether I like it or not, let me make a virtue of necessity and put no obstacles in the way.

Lord, I give you my will freely, for I know by experience that the only thing to do is to surrender myself wholly to you. Do whatever you want with me.

I remember how you fulfilled the Father's will so perfectly in trials, sufferings, persecution, insults. I remember your agony in the garden and your death on the Cross.

When I see what the Father chose for you, his best Beloved, I ask that I may be gifted with the love I need to suffer whatever the Father wills for my own life.

I place myself in your hands, wanting you alone. Give yourself completely to me in return. I am yours. Dispose of me in whatever way you wish.

Give us this day our daily bread

Lord, help me to realize how much I need you every day. The Bread of Life is yourself, the greatest gift the Father could have given. Only by you can I be nourished. Only by you can I be sustained in my desire to live for the Father and accomplish his will in my own life as you did in yours.

In giving us yourself in this most holy Sacrament I discover that I can want for nothing. I can cease being anxious about material necessities, for in you I have the one thing necessary – yourself.

This Sacrament with which you feed me is a healing for my whole person, body and soul. It is as if you were with me in the same way and, indeed, even more so than if I were able to see you with my bodily eyes during the time you lived on earth.

When you come to me in Holy Communion it is as if you were entering my house and allowing me to remain with you as did Mary Magdalen. In the Blessed Sacrament I know by faith that you are within me, and what closer union could there be than that?

Give me grace to know who you really are and to receive you with love, not just for my personal comfort but for the whole Church. In giving back to the Father the gift he has given me, the gift of his own Son, surely my prayers for the Church cannot go unheeded but will bear fruit for all.

And forgive us our trespasses as we forgive those who trespass against us
Lord, you ask us to forgive others as we ourselves are forgiven by you. I have so much to be forgiven. So little to forgive by comparison.

In the past I used to feel slighted and hurt over nothing, I was so sensitive. Now, dear Lord, I have a greater sense of my own sinfulness, so I come to you with empty hands, wanting only your pardon and the grace to live in love and peace with all. Teach me how to suffer wrongs with patience. Give me fortitude.

Prayer which does not result in forgiveness of others is not true prayer at all. You are everything, I am nothing. You have forgiven me so much how can I possibly dare to withold forgiveness from anyone?

And lead us not into temptation but deliver us from evil.

Lord, help me to be always ready for the hour of conflict, knowing that your strength within me will overcome all evil. Let me be always intent upon pleasing you, serving you, keeping near to you. Of myself I am weak but in you I can do all things.

Take from me all vain self-trust that I may place all my trust in you. I know that without you I cannot be holy, that without you I fall a thousand times a day.

Teach me to draw profit from the times I fall and not sink into depression or despair. Give me the humility which knows how to rely on you and thus win the victory.

Let me not succumb to the pride which causes inner disquiet. Teach me to remain trustingly with you in peace, joy and tranquillity even when I become more and more aware of my own sins.

You are the Merciful One. I do not trust in my own strength but in your mercy. Help me at every moment. Never let me give up prayer which keeps me in touch with you. Help me to desire only what is good, true and beautiful.

This prayer of the Our Father is enough for me, Lord. It teaches me all I need to know, for the words come from your own lips.

Blessed and praised may you be, for from you comes all the good that we speak, think or do. Amen.

For Reflection

1. Teresa stresses the need for a balanced life style which gives sufficient time to prayer, work, recreation and relationships with others. Consider your own life and think what may need adjustment in order to foster all the elements she considers important.

2. Love of God and love of neighbour are intimately related. Make some definite resolution to go out to another and to offer help wherever it is needed.

3. Teresa never left prayer time to chance. Deepen your love for Scripture so that you have something to nourish your thoughts on if they are inclined to wander. Have some other book on hand which will help you prepare your mind and heart as you approach God.

4. Follow Teresa's method for reflecting on the Our Father, using it for some favourite prayer or hymn of your own choosing. Write down what comes to you so that you can return to it later.

5. 'Forgive as we forgive.' Is there some area in your life where you are hanging on to past hurts? Ask for the grace to forgive others as the Lord forgives you, continually and completely.

NOTES
  1 *The Interior Castle*, Mansion 5, 1:2
  2 *Way of Perfection*, 4:4
  3 Matthew 25:40
  4 John 13:34–35
  5 *The Interior Castle*, Mansion 5, 3:9
  6 *Ibid*, 3:11
  7 *Ibid*, Mansion 3, 2:14
  8 Matthew 7:5
  9 *Life*, 13:11
 10 *Way of Perfection*, 10:3

11 *The Interior Castle*, Mansion 1, 2:9
12 *Ibid*, 6:10
13 John 5:44
14 *Life*, 31:20
15 Matthew 12:33
16 *Way of Perfection*, 12:8
17 *Ibid*, 21:4
18 *Life*, 4:7
19 *Way of Perfection*, 32:2
20 John 4:7–15
21 *Life*, 30:10
22 Matthew 6:9–13
23 This section is a free adaptation of chapters 26–40 of the *Way of Perfection*

Chapter 3

The Praying Person – St John of the Cross

John of the Cross (1542–91) was born in Fontiveros, a village on the Castilian plateau, and died at Ubeda in southern Spain forty-nine years later. His childhood was spent in great poverty and he had to struggle hard to find time for the basic education which enabled him to enter the Carmelite Order in Medina del Campo when he was twenty-one. As part of his priestly formation, John attended courses at the University of Salamanca where he was considered a brilliant student. A sound theological and philosophical formation undergirds all his writings on the spiritual life.

At the age of twenty-five, when John was considering a transfer to the Carthusian Order where he thought his attraction to prayer and solitude would have more scope for development, he was introduced to Teresa of Avila by a friend. The fifty-two-year-old Teresa was hoping to begin a reformed branch of Carmelite friars to complement her nuns and she saw in John an ideal collaborator. John decided forthwith to give himself to the project she had in mind and was the first to do so.

Always a quiet and personally austere man, John suffered much at the hands of both groups of friars, even enduring a period of harsh imprisonment at Toledo in an effort to force him to abandon the Reform. In his subsequent career John held a variety of offices in the Order: as superior, Provincial counsellor, novice-master, lecturer and preacher. He was also much sought after as a spiritual director by both nuns and lay people. Posterity recognizes in John a major poet of the Spanish language despite his small output.

John speaks to us now in the priory garden of Los Martires, Granada. He has taken a great interest in this site, helping to build an aquaduct to provide water for the plants as well as the friars. From our vantage point above the city he points out the magnificent view of the surrounding countryside which so obviously feeds the spirit of this gentle and sensitive man. He is an accomplished director and speaks with earnestness and sincerity in a soft, but firm, tone of voice. From time to time his features light up with a shy smile that transforms his whole face. Small in height, slight in build, with a balding head, he could easily be overlooked in a group. But on his own one feels oneself to be in the presence of a man who has truly experienced what his poems describe.

John Speaks

Love has always been the pivotal reality of my life and I see the love of God for each person as something sacred and life-giving. Everything I see around me speaks of God's love – the beautiful scenery, my relationships with others, food, drink, religious and community celebrations; all have deep roots in a love beyond anything we can fully experience on earth. These verses from the *Spiritual Canticle* sing of a reality in which I believe with all my heart:

> *My Beloved is the mountains,*
> *The solitary wooded valleys,*
> *The strange islands,*
> *The roaring torrents,*
> *The whisper of the amorous winds,*
>
> *The tranquil night*
> *At the approaches of the dawn,*
> *The silent music,*
> *The murmuring solitude,*
> *The supper which revives and enkindles love.*
>
> *My soul is occupied,*
> *And all my substance in his service;*
> *Now I guard no flock,*
> *Nor have I any other employment:*
> *My sole occupation is love.*[1]

I interpret God's love for humanity as a marriage covenant, Jesus taking the human race as bride through the consent of Mary, Carmel's principal patron. She is the image of each faithful person who responds to the invitation to intimacy that God offers. In her I see what the human person is called to be and to become.

Everyone's picture of God is coloured by their own personal history. The Scriptures say that God is love;[2] and the costliness of human love, its power, its passion, its ability to inspire sacrifice in the lover, were all instilled into me from a very early age.

When my father met my mother, Catalina, she was a poor orphan while he came from a well-to-do family. But they fell in love and my father, Gonzalez, gave up everything to marry her. His family were so horrified they cut him off with nothing and he had to earn a living helping my mother do piece-work weaving. We lived in the greatest poverty but there was love in our home. My father never regretted his choice though he died young from overwork and privation when I was barely seven. That left my mother alone as the breadwinner with three young sons to support. Luis, the middle boy, died of starvation, and Francisco, the eldest, and I moved with mother from place to place as she struggled to find work. My mother and brother are my greatest treasures. We have gone through so much together, and my mother has sacrificed herself for my education and happiness when it would have been easier for her to care only for herself.

I understand that love is the supreme motivating force of the human person and that is why, even in my worst hours, I've tried to discover the hand of God present and leading me, albeit often in darkness and pain.

When I was imprisoned in Toledo I had to escape by night from my tormentors, yet I saw even in this an image and symbol of the costly journey of love that ends in union after all obstacles are overcome:

> *Upon a darksome night,*
> *Kindling with love in flame of yearning keen,*
> *– O moment of delight –*
> *I went by all unseen,*
> *New-hush'd to rest the house where I had been.*

O night that leds't me thus!
O night more winsome than the rising sun!
O night that madest us,
Lover and lov'd as one,
Lover transformed in lov'd, Love's journey
done.[3]

We have to think of this only: that *all is ordained by*
God, and where there is no love put love, and we will
draw love out.[4]

The Mount of Carmel

A simple way in which I put down my approach to
the question of how to love God and attain union
with him is contained in this sketch of the mountain
of Carmel which I drew for the nuns of Beas. If
Carmel is a mountain whose summit is union with
God then you have to take the straight path with no
deviations. Just as my father decided, when he
wanted to marry my mother, that he would brook no
obstacle others tried to place in his way, that
nothing would deflect him from his purpose, so the
path to God is one in which we let nothing take us
away from the One we love above all else. With St
Paul we can say in truth 'I want to know nothing
but Christ and the power of his resurrection. I have
thrown everything else away and count it as
nothing, as so much rubbish, if only I can have
Christ and be found in him. I am racing for the
finish, for the prize of the upward call of God in
Christ Jesus.'[5]

On the summit of the mountain you'll see there is
nothing but the honour and glory of God, and one
travels there only by way of Christ and the imitation of him in his earthly life. The path traced for us
by the Gospels is the only way, and it is a narrow

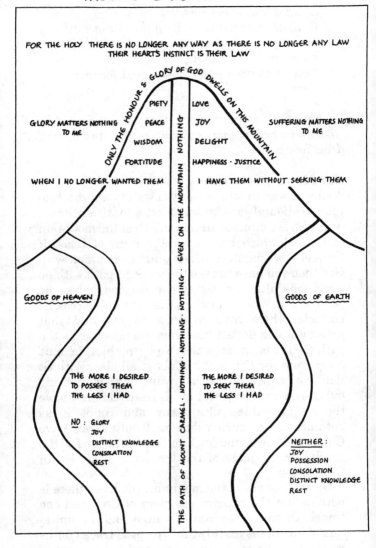

FOR THE HOLY THERE IS NO LONGER ANY WAY AS THERE IS NO LONGER ANY LAW
THEIR HEART'S INSTINCT IS THEIR LAW

ONLY THE HONOUR & GLORY OF GOD DWELLS ON THIS MOUNTAIN

PIETY   LOVE
GLORY MATTERS NOTHING   PEACE   JOY   SUFFERING MATTERS NOTHING
TO ME   WISDOM   DELIGHT   TO ME
FORTITUDE   HAPPINESS · JUSTICE

WHEN I NO LONGER WANTED THEM   I HAVE THEM WITHOUT SEEKING THEM

NOTHING

GOODS OF HEAVEN   GOODS OF EARTH

THE PATH OF MOUNT CARMEL · NOTHING · NOTHING · NOTHING · EVEN ON THE MOUNTAIN

THE MORE I DESIRED   THE MORE I DESIRED
TO POSSESS THEM   TO SEEK THEM
THE LESS I HAD   THE LESS I HAD

NO : GLORY   NEITHER :
JOY   JOY
DISTINCT KNOWLEDGE   POSSESSION
CONSOLATION   CONSOLATION
REST   DISTINCT KNOWLEDGE
          REST

way, one you have to choose consciously.[6] It doesn't just 'happen' that you find it. *Consider the great and significant import of the word 'how' in 'how narrow is the gate'. It is as if the Lord said 'In truth it is much narrower than you think. Those who wish to enter it must therefore be ready to lay aside all that is not God. He alone is to be loved above everything.'*[7]

Life hinges upon desire, for we are creatures of desire. If we have God we have everything. If we allow ourselves to be enslaved by other things our desires are 'split off' from the one thing necessary and run hither and thither, restless and unsatisfied. Giving up things isn't the point, having the disposition to give up anything that hinders us on the Godward path is.

I can't emphasize this sufficiently because many people seem to think that union with God depends on special gifts. It doesn't. It depends on what we really want. If we want God we shall have him. If we want something else that is what we will get. But in God we actually do have all, strange as that may sound. I've found true happiness and can say: *the heavens are mine, the earth is mine; mine the just and mine the sinners. Mine are the angels and the Mother of God. And all things are mine. God himself is mine and for me, because Christ is mine and all for me. What do you ask for then, what seek for, my soul? Everything is yours. Do not be satisfied with the crumbs which fall from the table of the Father. Go forth, exult in your glory, hide yourself in it and you shall obtain all that your heart desires.*[8]

Beginning the Ascent
Before anyone starts out on the road to union with God, God awakes a desire for this within the heart.

41

It is a desire to go beyond the ego and its circum-scribed world, and venture into the reality beyond. One 'wants' to climb the mountain and not remain earthbound. I call this initial wanting a 'wound' of love. It makes us restless, ready to begin the search. It is a sure sign that we have been touched by God. We long for him yet he is hidden. *Seeing that the Bridegroom you love is the 'treasure hidden in the field'[9] of your soul for which the wise merchant gave all that he had; so you, if you want to find the Lord, must forget and withdraw from all created things and pray to the Father in secret.[10] Courage then, for the One you love, the only One who can heal your wound, dwells within you and invites you to intimacy.[11]*

Each human person is made for God, each has a capacity for transcendence, union with the Divine. But God is Mystery, and in great part we are a mystery to ourselves. *We are called then to pass courageously beyond our natural limits and enter into Mystery. To do this we need faith, and faith is darkness. It means believing without seeing. It is 'night' to our senses.[12]*

The ego curls inwards on itself, drawing every-thing in to destroy it like a carniverous flower, while the true self has little opportunity to come into its own. We are naturally self-seeking, self-protective. Yet we are called to a destiny beyond ourselves. How sad then to look for fulfilment in transitory things, even when we know intellectually that they cannot afford lasting satisfaction.

Creation in itself is good and beautiful. It is humans who pervert it by using it merely for their own personal pleasure or profit. If in faith we step out in obedience to the call of God everything else will fall into proper perspective.

The search, the ascent, however you want to describe it, means gradually leaving the ego in order to find the true self, and to find it where it really is, in God. That demands that we do what we can, show God our serious intent so that in due time he will take over the process and do the work we cannot possibly do of ourselves. On our side, we have to practise meditation so that we grow in faith and in conviction through pondering on eternal truth as far as we can; and we have to undertake a real asceticism.

Asceticism can sound a challenging word but all it means is that *we have to make efforts to advance, for if we would find God it is not enough to pray with the tongue and have recourse to the help of others. We must work ourselves according to our powers, for God values our efforts. A genuine love of and desire for God is not content with words alone. It demands action.*[13]

The actions I am speaking of are not so much specific deeds as they are to do with basic attitudes of self-denial which turn much of our thinking upside-down. After all, you have to *have* something before you can give it up. You have to *be* a person before God can transform you as a person. We tend to assume that some activities are specifically God-centred and some are sinful. In embarking on the imitation of Christ which is the ground of all holiness, I remind people that *every satisfaction offered to the senses which is not for the honour and glory of God must be renounced.*[14] But you must have known some satisfaction first. It is all too easy to think that prayer, purity, discipline and other things costly to human nature are to be fostered, and sinful things avoided, while assuming there is a whole area of neutrality that has nothing to do with God and fills most of our day: work, leisure, meals, relationships, reading, gardening, culture in all its forms. We need these. They are God's gifts, to be used rightly and appreciated.

There is no such things as neutrality; either we are acting for God's honour and glory or we are not. God comes to us through many areas of created reality that we dismiss as irrelevant. I don't want people to be fearful of lovely pictures, good reading, the satisfaction afforded by friendship and marriage. Only the Beloved could have created and nurtured all these wonderful gifts that enrich our lives. *Considering the creation the soul is profoundly stirred to love God the Beloved, for it recognizes all as the work of his hands.*[15] Jesus came that we might have fulness of life, and not be timid and fearful as if evil were lurking around every corner.

However, it is natural for us to use things and people in an ego-centric way; that's why I counsel labouring for purity of vision, of hearing, touching, tasting. It's important that we turn aside from anything that does not help us grow in the love of God and instead turns us inwards in a selfish way. Often in practice it is the love and service of others which determines what we must deny ourselves. Our aim is not freedom from emotion but emotional freedom, and ultimately joy in all things.

The Meaning of Peace and Freedom
Everything I have said and written is meant to help people be free of the tyranny of the ego. That means choosing: choosing to see or turn away, to hear or not to listen, to follow our baser instincts or channel them in another direction. Everything depends on our will, our choice. By choosing we make ourselves into a certain kind of person. That's why it helps our

choices to be the right ones if we look always at Jesus, the perfect expression of the Father for us. It is Jesus who summons us beyond our human boundaries into the greatness of the Father's world – complete trust in him, not ourselves.

Naturally we are our own horizon. To me I am the most important person in the universe. To begin ascending the mountain you have to make a decision against self-importance. Think little of yourself, be prepared to be hidden. Believe in the love of God and you'll gradually be able to rely on the Lord and not on passing fame or acclamation. Everything will be unified in God. You'll be able to say truthfully *'My sole occupation is love.' All I do is done in love; all I suffer I suffer in the sweetness of love.*[16] Whatever is your particular struggle for freedom, and in this temperaments differ, you'll be glad in the end when freedom is yours.

This is the point where prayer comes in. Without God we really can't do anything. We just have to wait on God's time, believing that we will receive refreshment when we need it. Wanting other things (those unruly desires again!) wears us out in the long run. *Unruly desires resemble little children, restless and dissatisfied, wanting now one thing, now another. They are never content. Anyone interested only in money tires themselves out digging for gold. Those who pursue their desires, and even obtain what they think they want, end in weariness. They are never satisfied.*[17]

Peace, which is what we really desire at the deepest level of our being, flows from contact with the Spirit of God. 'Come to me, all you who labour and are heavily burdened and I will refresh you,' says the Lord.[18] *It is as if Jesus said, 'All you who are tormented and afflicted, labouring beneath the*

45

burden of anxiety and desire, cast it aside by coming to me and I will refresh you. In me alone shall your souls find the rest of which your desires rob you.'[19]

Does it make any difference whether a bird is held by a slender thread or a rope? Whatever holds it back means it cannot fly freely.[20] It is so sad to see good people held back from union with God by mere nothings, which they cannot relinquish. Love would make it so much easier, a love borne of prayer and attachment to Christ, a love which accepts ourselves as valuable people with a divine destiny. We don't have to be 'perfect'. Faith tells us that God is within us and inviting us to a life of love, no matter who we are or where we are on the road.

O soul, most beautiful of creatures, who long so earnestly to know the place where your Beloved is that you may seek and be united to him. You are yourself the very tabernacle where he dwells, the secret room in which he is hidden. Rejoice then and be glad, because all your good and all your hope is so near you as to be within you. 'You are the temple of the living God.'[21] *What joy for the soul to learn that God never abandons it even in serious sin, how much less when it is in a state of grace? What more is there to look for when your Beloved is with you and within you.'*[22]

The Desert and the Night

I've written a lot about the 'night' in which one who seeks God has to persevere in darkness and faith. It's rather like the desert through which God led the Israelites to the Promised Land. In the desert they learned to rely on the Lord and not on their own resources. As prayer develops, as we get closer to God, we experience the pain of discovering and standing in our own truth. It is painful to come

46

before God just as we are in all our poverty and nakedness; and the nearer we get to God the more we are aware of it. It's the easiest and the hardest thing to do – just to remain there with all our deficiencies and hangups, and not pretend to be the good, pious people we would like to be, but rather accepting the people we actually are.

My teaching can make deep demands on others because I have understood through my own life experience that God wants to bring us to close union, and coming close to God simultaneously purifies and transforms us. It's like fire which turns what it touches into itself. God hollows out places within us that we never knew even existed. We are stretched by suffering to enlarge our capacity for bearing pain, and nobody likes that part. But we also enlarge our capacity for joy – and that shouldn't be forgotten either. It's the transition from childishness to adult childlikeness that any committed Christian has to go through in one way or another.

The Dark Night is really one continuous process of purification when we are tested to see whether we are serious in our desire for God or just interested in spiritual 'experiences' which make us feel good about ourselves.

You see, in meditating on the life of Jesus, in trying to live virtuous lives, we are doing a lot of work (and necessary, indispensible work). But we can't attain holiness under our own steam, that's a divine work. Mystical prayer, the 'dark night', means that God has to take over. It is *God* who leads us into the night and prepares us to receive him on his own terms – the terms of grace, not merit. We have to hand over the control of our life to God.

At first, *when a soul is seriously converted to God, it is, in general, spiritually nursed and caressed, as an infant by its loving mother. She warms it at her breast, nourishes it with her own sweet milk, feeds it with tender and delicate food, carries it in her arms and fondles it. But as the child grows up the mother witholds her caresses, hides her breasts and anoints them with bitter aloes. She carries the infant in her arms no longer but makes it walk on the ground so that, losing the habits of an infant, it may apply itself to greater and more substantial pursuits.*[23]

Usually God leads us at first in the ways of sweetness because we are so tiny and unformed in the ways of virtue. Prayer is attractive and pleasurable to us, and we think we are doing well. We may even be tempted to look down on others. So God has to take us in hand and test us. Then we realize that we too are weak – indeed even weaker than we thought possible. What a grace! Now we can pray in truth 'Lord, be merciful to me a sinner.'

God and the Self

Contact *with* God deflates us. Ideas *about* God boost us. Self-seeking in the spiritual life is a canker that has to be destroyed. It's a question of getting beyond our self-image to reach true self-knowledge and these are often confused in people's minds. Self-knowledge is a true appreciation of self with our strong and weak points acknowledged and held in tension. Our self-image is illusory and it's this which exerts such a hold over us. If we cannot let our self-image go, God cannot lead us into deep prayer as he wishes to. The simple reason is that prayer is a relationship, and no one can relate to an image but only to a person – a real person.

As self-knowledge and prayer go hand in hand, so our self-knowledge deepens along with our prayer. Self-knowledge is to do with the truth of who we are; it engenders humility *ipso facto*. Our self-image is illusory and leads to pride (which we can mistake for humility, especially if our self-image is a poor one).

We can't see ourselves objectively, that's why the picture (or image) we have of ourselves is built up on how others see us, primarily our parents or other significant adults, in childhood. We receive our self-image through osmosis. Did our parents tell us we were awkward and incompetent? That will be the image we form of ourselves. Did they tell us we were not good looking and would find it hard to get a life-partner on that account? Sure enough, we'll pick that up too. Alternatively, did they tell us we were wonderful, better than everyone else as long as we did what pleased them? None of these observations are necessarily objective truth. We are most likely perfectly competent and presentable, but that is not how we believe ourselves to be. Our self-knowledge is hampered by our poor (or vastly overrated) self-image.

Maturity involves a more objective looking at self. It means opening out in trust to the perceptions and suggestions that come to us from elsewhere. It means going forward in trust – trust that God sees and loves the real person I am beneath the veneer. So I allow him to peel away the protective layers.

An image cannot follow Jesus, only a person can do that. An image isn't open to relationships, to community, to genuine love. All we can see when we are living in our 'image' is a reflection of ourselves that we have become used to, but which is actually reflected back from a distorted mirror – ourselves as

49

we think others see us. To face the truth when we have been used to living in untruth is to face chaos – the dark night – and the possibility of painful change. Only God can introduce us to this kind of truth because only God can uphold us and give us courage. Only he can teach us our true value.

Prayer doesn't reward us with a better self-image – that's just looking for 'rewards' that are worthless, as if God will repay our services with good feelings about ourselves just because we have renounced other kinds of attachments. God will reward us with the *truth*: we are loved, we are precious *and* we are sinners for whom Christ died, upheld and loved in all our tears and pain and joy. Seeking God, loving God is its own reward. Nothing, nothing, nothing, in order to attain the All that is found in him alone.

Have you ever wanted the stigmata, some special vision, some special 'touch' of God's love to prove his choice of you? Forget it! Everything we need is right here in Jesus and in the Gospel, for *in giving us his Son, who is the Word, God has spoken to us once and for all and has nothing further to reveal.*[24]

Contemplating Christ Crucified

And so I come back to where I began – the contemplation of Jesus who went the narrow way of the cross. To choose him is to choose the cross, the chalice, self-denial. *Anything else is seeking self in God instead of seeking God as he is.*[25]

Christ who is our Way experienced the agony and abandonment of Calvary at the supreme moment of our redemption. This is what is means to die of love. It is this selfless love we are called to partake of. So the way to union with Jesus is not by acquiring possessions, even spiritual ones, not by building ourselves up but by letting everything go. It is complete self-dispossession, absolute freedom and joy because there is no longer an image to protect. One walks in truth with Truth itself.

In the freedom won for us, the freedom of love, I can now say that *'my sole occupation is love'. All I do is done in love. All I suffer I suffer in the sweetness of love. This is the meaning of David in the psalms: 'I will keep my strength for you.'*[26] Union with Christ is the most important thing on earth, the only thing that brings ultimate satisfaction and peace. It is the end of persevering prayer. It is the fulfilment of love. And *one instant of pure love is more precious in the eyes of God and the soul, and more profitable to the Church than all other good works together, though it may seem that nothing were done.*[27]

For Reflection

1. Look at the sketch of the Mountain of Carmel and ponder on John's teaching about taking the direct route. Are there ways in which you yourself are following the winding paths that lead nowhere? Ask the Lord to give you the grace you need to want nothing but him.

2. John loved the image of the night and darkness. Light a candle and sit quietly pondering on the words of Isaiah: 'My soul has desired you in the night; my spirit within me earnestly seeks you.'

3. Spend some time in contemplating (looking at) a crucifix that appeals to you. Here we see what it means to love and abandon oneself to God completely. Make some personal acts of love and abandonment to Christ Crucified.

4. Write down a list of the things people have told you about yourself when you were young. Are they objectively true now? Ask God to give you

real self-knowledge instead of a distorted self-image, the ability to see yourself as you are in God's eyes – his beloved child.

5. John's conception of love owed a lot to his childhood experience. How has your picture of God been dependent on your family and upbringing? Is this in any way contrary to the picture Jesus gives of his Father in the Gospels?

NOTES
1 *The Spiritual Canticle*, 14, vv. 15, 28
2 1 John 4:16
3 *The Dark Night of the Sons*, vv. 1, 5 (Allison Peers' trans.)
4 Letter 16 to Mother Mary of the Incarnation, *Complete Works*, Volume 2
5 cf Philippians 3:7–13
6 Matthew 7:14
7 *The Ascent of Mount Carmel*, Bk 2, 7:1
8 Prayer of an Enamoured Soul, *Complete Works*, Volume 2
9 Matthew 13:44
10 Matthew 6:6
11 *The Spiritual Canticle*, 1:8
12 *The Ascent of Mount Carmel*, Bk 2, 3:3
13 *The Spiritual Canticle*, 3:2
14 *The Ascent of Mount Carmel*, Bk 1, 13:4
15 *The Spiritual Canticle*, 4:5
16 *Ibid*, 28:8
17 *The Ascent of Mount Carmel*, Bk 1, 6:3
18 Matthew 11:28
19 *The Ascent of Mount Carmel*, Bk 1, 8:4
20 *Ibid*, 11:5
21 2 Corinthians 6:16
22 *The Spiritual Canticle*, 1:7
23 *The Dark Night of the Soul*, Bk 1, 1:2
24 *The Ascent of Mount Carmel*, Bk 2, 12:13
25 *Ibid*, 7:3
26 *The Spiritual Canticle*, 28:8
27 *Ibid*, 28:11

Chapter 4

Walking in God's Presence – Brother Lawrence

Brother Lawrence of the Resurrection (Nicolas Herman) was born in Lorraine about the year 1691. He had a chequered background, spending some time as a soldier, then as a footman. On several occasions he attempted life as a hermit but his instability made him realize that he needed a more structured religious life; so in middle age he offered himself to the Carmelite community in Paris as a lay-brother. The following 30 years were spent in the kitchen where he gradually became known for his holiness of life and his approachability. Numerous men and women of all classes, clerical and lay, sought his help, asking him to share with them the secret of his almost continual prayer.

The little book which contains a record of the conversations, letters and maxims of Brother

Lawrence, entitled *The Practice of the Presence of God*, has become a classic in both Catholic and Protestant circles.

Brother Lawrence was never canonized but he continues to influence many by his simple and direct approach, based on the practical experience of a busy person.

We can picture him now in his kitchen, surrounded by steaming pots of vegetables. He is a big, raw-boned man with a plain, coarse-featured face. He walks with a pronounced limp, due to an injury sustained when he was a soldier. His manner is courteous and he smiles readily. The dents in the cooking utensils witness to a certain clumsiness – he is forever dropping things or bumping into them unawares – but his placid good nature is unperturbed by his ham-handedness. He sits at a table peeling swedes, then chopping them and placing them deliberately in a prepared basin as he speaks. His brown habit is protected by a large, rough apron of sacking on which the vegetable peelings fall from time to time. He flicks them on to the floor with an amused grin.

Brother Lawrence Speaks

I expect every family, every parish and every religious community has its odd-bods, and Carmel is no exception. In fact, I think it's a sign of good health when unusual types can be incorporated into the common enterprise without being wrenched out of shape. I'm one of those odd-bods myself and I'm very happy here nonetheless. I can be who I am simply and without disguise even though I'm a bit unusual.

I'm only a lay-brother after all, a 'nobody' who

joined up later in life. I work silently in the kitchen while there are a number of big-wigs among the priest friars always in demand for sermons, and out and about on various apostolic missions. It rather puts their noses out of joint when the fine people they address turn up later at the back door here, wanting to talk to me instead of them! I'm used to it now and take no notice, even though it can be a source of embarassment to the Prior. In fact, he leaves me a free hand – if God's work is done it doesn't matter who does it. God can pick and choose as he pleases and he seems to choose the unlikely candidate more often than not.

I'll tell you a bit about myself and how I came to be here at all. When I was eighteen years old and a soldier, I was laid up in bed recovering from a wound that's responsible for my lameness. It was winter. I happened then to notice a tree outside my window stripped of leaves. Suddenly it occurred to me that in spring those bare branches would sprout new buds, harbinger of flowers and fruit to follow, and I was overcome with a sense of God's power and providence. God can take what is old and withered and make it fruitful, not just once or twice but over and over again.

As I mulled over this I was filled with love for the God of new life and decided that henceforth my life would be his. Maybe that's why I was given the name Lawrence of the Resurrection when I came to Carmel, as a reminder that Christ's rising is a sign of the life and love of God which can never die.

After that conversion experience I had a number of different jobs in the big world outside, never rising very high because I was a clumsy oaf, always dropping things and a bit slow on the uptake. I even tried the hermit vocation but I soon realized I wasn't suited to total solitude. I heard that Carmelites had a hermit spirituality lived out in a community setting. One of my uncles was a friar and he put in a good word for me when I decided to ask about joining the Order, otherwise I would never have been accepted, I'm sure.

So much for being a hermit! I have set time for prayer and I work away in the friary kitchen. But I also have to go out quite a lot, searching for bargains in the market, travelling distances to purchase good wine and other commodities. Frenchmen like the pleasures of the table and the men here are no exception – why should they be? They're only human like everyone else in this great city of Paris. I get very little peace in this place. As for the hermit life – well, that's non-existent as far as I'm concerned! I'm over-run with folks who turn up at all hours wanting to talk to me. I try to be at their disposal as best I can and I look on them as sent by the Lord. It would be wrong to turn them away just because I personally like solitude.

What has helped me more than anything else in the midst of activity is to live continually in God's presence. Whether I'm at prayer 'proper'; whether I'm at work here or shopping in the town, God is with me and I am with him. That's my secret. Nothing outlandish there; it's available to everyone. It just takes a bit of practice to fix it in one's consciousness.

Work and Carmel
Work has always had a significant place in the spirituality of Carmel. When the first hermits settled on the holy mountain, one of their aims was the re-establishment of simple, ordinary work as an

integral part of daily life, contrasting with the hours that monks in large monasteries spent in elaborate liturgical celebrations.

Daily work was not considered antithetical to a life of prayer by the desert fathers and mothers. There's a story told about John the Little who one day said to an older brother: 'I want to be free from care and not to work but to worship God without interruption.' And he took off his robe and went into the desert. After staying there a week he returned to his brother. When he knocked on the door his brother asked without opening it, 'Who is it?' He replied, 'It's John, your brother.' The other brother said, 'John has become an angel and is not among people any more.' Then John begged to be let in and said, 'It's me.' But his brother did not answer and left him there in distress until the next morning when he finally opened the door and said, 'If you are a human being you have to work again in order to live.' Then John repented saying, 'Forgive me brother, for I was wrong.'[1]

When our Mother St Teresa inaugurated her Reform, she insisted on work for her nuns and friars as a witness to poverty. Indeed, our Rule tells us to give ourselves to work of some kind so that the devil will find us busy and thus be unable to pierce the defences of our soul.[2] It also quotes St Paul, who urged the Thessalonians to imitate his labour and not eat the bread of idleness.[3] I myself am the kind of worker the book of Sirach speaks of, who rely on their hands to make a living:

> Without them a city cannot be established,
> and people cannot sojourn there.
> Yet they are not sought out for the council of
> the people,

nor do they attain eminence in the public
assembly.
They do not sit in the judge's seat
nor do they understand the sentence of judgement,
and they are not found using proverbs.
But they keep stable the fabric of the world
and their prayer is in the practice of their
trade.[4]

Nobody asks my opinion when the brothers gather
to discuss the business of the community. I don't
have any voice in Chapter. My job is to keep the
kitchen stove going and to see that meals are served
on time. It's *practical* prayer.

Some people seem to have an idea that work is
demeaning, a 'second best' when one cannot do
much intellectually. I don't think so. St Paul says
the Church is a body in which everyone has their
own function, no one is more important than
anybody else.

> There are varieties of gifts but the same Spirit, there
> are varieties of service to be done but always the
> same Lord, and there are varieties of working, but it
> is the same God who inspires them all in everyone.
> To each is given the manifestation of the Spirit for
> the common good.[5]

It's the same in a Carmelite community which is a
'little church' just as a family is. Our Mother Teresa
understood this well. A family, a community, needs
Martha as well as Mary to function, so why should I
worry at having to work hard like I do? It helps
everyone, and nobody can survive on an empty
stomach, however holy. St Teresa writes:

Remember that there must be someone to cook the meals, and count yourselves happy in being able to serve like Martha. Reflect that true humility consists to a great extent in being ready for what the Lord desires to do with you and happy that he should do it, and in always considering yourselves unworthy to be his servants. If contemplation, and mental and vocal prayer and tending the sick and serving in the house and working at even the lowliest occupations are of service to the Guest who comes to stay with us and eat and take his recreation with us, what should it matter to us if we do one of these things rather than another? [6]

In fact, excessive solitude can be a snare because we kid ourselves that we have virtues we don't actually possess when we are left alone with no one bothering us.

My patience is continually tested here and I'm glad of it. I not only have to cook regular meals for the brothers, day in and day out, but there are unexpected callers, tramps who come looking for food and a chat by the fire, visitors for the Prior who will send for some tempting dish at short notice and so on ... and on ... It's my responsibility to see that everyone who comes gets a welcome, no matter what inconvenience that causes me. *I'm never scandalized by the wretchedness and sinfulness that others pour out to me. I pray for sinners, knowing that I'm one myself and I trust God to remedy everything in his own good time.* [7]

Work as a Form of Prayer

I didn't come to Carmel just to be a cook. I came to give myself completely to God in a life of prayer, which is why the Carmelite Order exists. So it was up to me to find a way to live continually in a state of prayer while accomplishing my duties. That's how I developed my method which consists solely of living continually in the presence of God whatever I may be doing.

Our great patron, the prophet Elijah, said that 'The Lord God lives, in whose presence I stand',[8] and the Virgin Mary too must have known herself to be always in God's presence as she went about her daily tasks. That's what I've tried to do by dint of long practice – live always in God's presence. It's the easiest and the hardest thing. And I stress again, it doesn't happen overnight. It takes practice before one becomes proficient.

I resolved, like John of the Cross, to make love the rule of all my actions without thinking about whether I would be lost or saved. *I was happy just to be able to pick up a straw out of love, wanting to please God alone with no ulterior motive whatsoever. I find, though, that God rewards me so quickly for the slightest thing that I wish I could hide my works from him so as to have the privilege of pleasing God without reward. I used to be worried over the state of my soul, should I go to heaven or hell? All that sort of thing. Now I never think along those lines. I let God do as he pleases and don't concern myself with anything else.*

When I began praying, my prayer consisted entirely in trying to overcome distractions and then falling into them again. All trouble begins in our thoughts. It's important to reject immediately anything that is unprofitable and unnecessary to whatever occupation we are engaged in and return our thoughts to God's presence. That is where alone we can find happiness.[9]

I've never been able to pray according to a pattern. I just try and cling on to God by faith and do everything for him. *If a good portion of time passes without my collecting myself in God's presence I don't belabour myself or fall into dejection. I just quietly return to him with more confidence than before. God is always honoured when we show trust, and he never allows one who truly trusts to be disappointed.*

When I work I think of what has to be done at the proper time, not worrying beforehand and anticipating difficulties, that wastes energy. Neither do I look back afterwards and go over everything again in my mind. What's past is past. Thus I find I am more united to God in my daily activities than I am at more formal times of prayer. In the beginning I found the discipline hard. It was an effort to act faithfully and renounce my own will; but after a while I found it easy and pleasant to do so. In times of difficulty we need only turn to Jesus and ask for his grace which makes all things sweet.[10]

I'm no scholar, no skilled practitioner in the spiritual life; just someone whose heart has been determined to turn to God only, to beat for him only, to love him only.

My prayer is simply realizing God's presence. It's a great delusion to think that prayer time should be different from any other time, for *we are equally bound to be united to God by work at work time as by prayer at prayer time.*[11]

Our Mother Teresa tells us that love of God is acquired by obedience to life and its real demands, so why should we tie God's hands by thinking there is only one way in which he can benefit us? Those who love God aren't anxious to preserve themselves in a selfish peace. If they see someone they can help they don't seek their own rest and comfort by ignoring a plea for assistance, even an unspoken plea. Instead they respond to what the Lord is obviously asking of them here and now, no matter how hard the labour involved. The highest perfection consists in doing God's will and doing it with alacrity and cheerfulness, for perfect love forgets itself in order to give pleasure to the Beloved.

It's more pleasant to be alone and left to yourself, and I certainly cherish solitude when I can get it; but if I can't, I don't fret. God is everywhere and not just hidden away in quiet corners where no one can get at me and call on my services.[12]

Our only concern in this life is to please God. Everything else is a waste of time. So let us turn in trust to the Father of Mercies who is always ready to receive us affectionately. Let us put our whole trust in God, praying unceasingly. But how can we pray to him unless we are often thinking of him? And how can we think of him often unless we make a habit of doing so? I know no better or easier way than this. The more we know God, the more we shall think of him and the more we shall love him.[13] So make a firm resolve never to forget him and remain always in his presence. *There is no life in the world happier than one of continual communion with God. If I were a preacher I would preach nothing else save the practice of the presence of God and recommend it to everyone, no matter who they are.*[14]

The Practice of the Presence of God[15]

Faith
Everything is possible to the person who believes, and those who are baptized and hold the faith have already taken the first steps on the way of perfection. They will become perfect insofar as they persevere in the following counsels:

We should refer to God and his glory in everything we do, say or undertake. This is to set ourselves to becoming true worshippers of God in this world. We must make a strong resolution to overcome, through grace, all difficulties which may hinder our spiritual growth.

We must firmly believe that such difficulties are part of God's providence and submit our minds and hearts to his will in love and with a patient spirit.

We must depend completely on grace at every moment, for without grace we can do nothing.

Practices for Attaining the Spiritual Life
The most holy and necessary practice of the spiritual life is that of the presence of God. In it we find joy and contentment. By it we can talk lovingly and humbly to him at all times without any particular rule or system, especially when we are troubled or tempted to have fallen into sin or unfaithfulness.

We should try to allow each action to become a moment of communion with God. This is not a studied accomplishment but one which springs from purity and simplicity of heart.

We must act in a calm and thoughtful manner, lovingly asking God to accept all we do and eschewing an haphazard approach to labour. During work and all activities – be they reading, study, devotions or prayers – we should stop frequently for a few moments to turn to God within us and, as it were by stealth, touch him as he passes.

Pause often to praise, thank, and adore him who dwells within you continually. These moments of recollection will purify you of self-seeking and self-love.

All these acts of worship must be the fruit of faith; faith that God truly dwells in our hearts, that he is the source of life, that he watches over us, that we are called to belong entirely to him. We should grow in self-knowledge, understanding our strong points and our weak points, and making it our custom to turn trustfully to God in all temptation, speaking to him with the intimacy that befits the One who is our greatest friend.

How We Must Worship God in Spirit and in Truth
God must be worshipped in the depths of our soul which he alone can see. With practice it will seem that God becomes one with the soul and the soul becomes one with God.

To worship God in truth is to recognize that God is who God is and we are what we are. Is it not unreasonable, therefore, not to use all our powers in serving and worshipping him?

To worship God in truth is also to admit that although God would like to form us in his image we separate ourselves from him. It is foolish then to withhold from him even a moment of our time and devotion.

Of the Union of the Soul with God
In actual union the soul is active, not passive, kindling light and warmth continually through her actions. This is not something dependent on feelings but has deeper roots in one's being. It impels the soul to love God peacefully and worship him unceasingly. Choosing God's will at all times is the greatest act of love, bringing with it freedom and peace.

Of the Presence of God
The practice of the presence of God is to apply our mind, imagination or understanding to him, realizing that he is present. It may be a loving gaze,

a silent conversation, a patient waiting, a peaceful repose. By repeated acts and by frequently recalling the mind to God, the soul becomes accustomed to turn Godwards when free from occupations and even in the midst of duties. It is as if God and the soul were alone and in communion with one another continually.

This communion is held in the depths of the soul where one speaks to God heart to heart. God's love thus kindles a fire in the soul and enables a loving conversation to proceed without hindrance, giving life and nourishment to one who rests in the divine presence.

Means for Attaining the Presence of God
The first means is great purity of life. The second is great fidelity to the practice of God's presence and in keeping the soul's gaze upon God quietly and humbly, lovingly eschewing all worry.

Take care to begin, continue and complete all your actions with an inward lifting of the heart to God. Do not be discouraged when this habit takes time to acquire. Your joy will be all the greater when you eventually succeed. It is a matter of the heart rather than the intellect, training it to turn spontaneously to the Lord at all times.

It is helpful to use short ejaculatory prayers such as 'My God, I am wholly yours', 'My God, I love you with all my heart', 'Lord, make my heart like your own', or any similar words which love may suggest. This practice is not easy to begin with, but if persevered in it leads to a simple gaze of love and is a source of unending grace. To recall God's presence is the most real, the most simple and the most fruitful kind of prayer. In this a certain control of the senses is taken for granted.

Benefits of the Presence of God
Faith becomes more active and more alive. Hope is
strengthened and encouraged by our growing
knowledge, as faith enables us to penetrate God's
mysteries more deeply. Love burns to ashes what is
contrary to love in the soul.

Almost all of life is thus passed in acts of love and
worship, trust, gratitude, contrition, and all the
virtues. This way of prayer prepares us for the
prayer of simple regard should God choose to give it.

For Reflection

1. What do you find most helpful in Brother
   Lawrence's teaching? Can you identify with his
   approach to work as helping rather than
   hindering us in our prayer if it is undertaken in
   the right spirit?
2. Choose some ejaculatory prayers that will help
   you turn your heart Godwards in the course of
   the day. Resolve to say them frequently and so
   build up a habit of continual prayer.
3. Ponder on St Teresa's famous maxim that 'God
   walks among the pots and pans'. Is there some
   area of your own life where he is not allowed to
   walk? Ask for light to see where and how Jesus
   can be invited into every place, within and
   without, in your life.
4. Keep a small notebook handy with thoughts that
   strike you: Scripture passages, favourite hymns,
   etc. When you have a spare moment re-read
   some of them to help you turn back to God and
   recall his presence.
5. 'God loves a cheerful giver.' How can you spread
   a little joy in the way you serve, rather than
   behaving like a martyr when things get difficult?

NOTES

1 *Desert Wisdom*, Yushi Nomura, Doubleday, 1984, p. 12
2 Rule no. 17
3 2 Thessalonians 3:7–12
4 Sirach 38:31–34 (NRSV)
5 1 Corinthians 12:4–7
6 *Way of Perfection*, St Teresa of Avila, 17:6
7 Conversation 1, *The Practice of the Presence of God*, Brother Lawrence, trans. D. Attwater, Burns and Oates, 1931
8 1 Kings 18:15
9 Conversation 2, Brother Lawrence, op. cit
10 Conversation 3, ibid
11 Conversation 4, ibid
12 The thoughts expressed in this and the previous paragraph are based on St Teresa's *Book of Foundations*, chapter 5
13 Letter 9, Brother Lawrence, op. cit
14 Letter 2, ibid
15 This section is based on Brother Lawrence's *Spiritual Maxims*

The Practice of the Presence of God contains the conversations, letters and maxims of Brother Lawrence.

Chapter 5

Knowing the God We Pray to – St Thérèse of Lisieux

Thérèse Martin, termed the greatest saint of modern times, was born in 1873, the youngest of nine children, of whom five survived, all girls. Thérèse's mother died of breast cancer when Thérèse was four and she was brought up by her father and older sisters in a secure and loving home, where religion played an important part in daily life. Very shy and sensitive following the trauma of her mother's death, with a pronounced piety from her earliest years, Thérèse asked for, and eventually obtained, permission to enter the Carmelite Convent in her home town of Lisieux at the age of fifteen, where two of her older sisters had already preceded her as nuns.

In this Carmel, while living in a manner that was outwardly very constrained and limited,

Thérèse came to great holiness. The story of her life and insights on the way of spiritual childhood were contained in three manuscripts she wrote for her sisters (manuscripts A, B and C). Collected in one volume and published in an edited version shortly after her death, the book (*The Story of a Soul*) literally took the Catholic world by storm. This provincial French girl had penetrated to the core of the Gospel in a unique way and was able to convince numerous people that sanctity really was within the grasp of anyone who wanted it enough, as she had done.

Thérèse died of tuberculosis at the age of twenty-four. In the short space of nine years in Carmel she had sought and found the truth – that God is a God of mercy and he asks only for love from those he has created and redeemed. The only response then is to give oneself completely to God in total confidence without counting the cost; not trusting in one's own merits but in the merciful love of the Lord who chooses 'little ones' to confound the powerful.

Thérèse speaks to us now sitting in a wicker wheelchair that once belonged to her father. She is relaxing beneath the trees of the chestnut avenue within the enclosure of the Lisieux Carmel. She is a tall young woman with fine features, a candid and open expression, grey eyes and a wide mouth. Within a few months she will be dead, as the TB is making rapid progress in her already emaciated frame. Her manner is simple and straightforward, and she speaks straight from the heart in a way unusual for a woman of the nineteenth-century French middle class.

Thérèse Speaks

My spirituality and my life are closely bound up together and everything I have said and written about springs from my experience, especially the experience of being a loved child. *All my first memories are of smiles and caresses.*[1] I knew I was loved and wanted to love others in return. How fortunate I was! I realize in retrospect that this was a special gift from the Lord who wanted to show me the power of love, rather than the pseudo power of fear, that so many associate with the motivating force behind religion. I was a happy, lively child, responsive to the beauties of nature and to all that was good.

This continued until I was four when Mama died and we moved house from Alençon to Lisieux so as to be near my cousins. My outgoing, happy disposition was changed completely by this bereavement; only within the family circle could I be myself. When I was sent to school for a while I became so unhappy I had to be withdrawn; I was a clever pupil but quite unable to mix with my peers. They thought I was just stuck-up and made my life miserable. I was bewildered by competitive games and petty rivalries – at home I was treated as if I were wrapped up in cotton wool, delicate and special – no wonder I couldn't cope like normal children! Only in the love of God could I expand and my First Communion was one of the happiest days of my life. I was flooded with grace – but my! – was I self-centred!

When my second sister Pauline, who had been a second mother to me, joined the convent I was totally devastated; so much so that I became seriously ill. It was as if my whole being was crying out in loneliness and anguish and I couldn't express

71

it. Can a child die of grief? I think I was close to it. Then it seemed as if a statue of Mary that was in my sick room smiled at me. I realized I *did* have a mother in Mary and gradually I got well again. One of the things that kept me going was the thought that one day I would join my sister in Carmel but I was so weepy and sensitive that it seemed like an impossible dream.

Being such a timid girl it was obvious that God would have to come in strongly with his grace. I had to be taken out of my self-preoccupation and given the courage to face life; that happened just before my fourteenth birthday. The Child of the Crib helped me to find once again that happy, outgoing child I had been before Mama's death; and from then on I never looked back. I had *tried*. That was enough for God. He then stepped in to do what I couldn't possibly do of my own accord – turned me outwards to think of others and forget myself.

With two older sisters now in Carmel I was determined to enter myself. *I felt it was the desert in which God wanted me to live so that I could belong to him alone,*[2] not for my own sake but to help others through my prayers and sacrifices. Eventually I was allowed to enter at fifteen – I even went to the Pope to try and get the permission needed for that. My goodness, I could be insufferable when I wanted my own way! The most difficult thing was saying goodbye to my father. I was his darling as the youngest, but he let me go with his blessing.

I certainly felt very special. Everyone I knew praised me for doing a wonderful thing at such a young age. I even thought I knew almost all there was to know about God and about love and life. I see now that I needed Carmel, not to provide a shelter from the world but to make me realize I was just as much a needy person as the worst sinner. Everyone lives from mercy, not merit.

The Acceptance of a Common Humanity

When I stepped over the threshold of the enclosure, I stepped into an environment where I was speedily forced to confront the person I really was by the very fact of living so closely with others of differing backgrounds and temperaments. My family had loved me and shielded me from so much that could have hurt my sensitivity. The sisters I met now were not about to treat me as a 'little queen' but as one of themselves who had to fit in with them and their idiosyncratic ways. So began the long struggle to come to terms with my own humanity, to experience it in the raw, so to speak, and to learn to accept others on their terms rather than on my own.

Instead of feeling that I was doing something wonderful for God, God seemed to have fled away. My prayer was dry as a bone. I couldn't work competently and was constantly criticized. I formed a passionate attachment to the prioress and had to struggle to master my feelings and attain a love that was free and mature, not like that of a dog for its owner. Above all, my adored father became mentally ill soon after my entrance and I was unable to communicate with him. Eventually he was taken away to an asylum and people said it was the loss of his youngest daughter that had affected his brain.

These things aren't heroic, the stuff of epic and song, they are the common lot of many, and I did not find myself coping in an heroic fashion either. Life could seem grim. Where were my beautiful feelings? The feelings I had had that God had chosen me,

73

that I was his child, his special beloved? That's when I determined to love God for himself, not for what I could get out of it, and I resolved to show it by loving my sisters at every opportunity that presented itself. I emerged from my dreams and began to face reality.

How did I show love? Well, in tiny things such as allowing a sister to splash me with dirty water when we were working together in the laundry; refusing to pass judgement when it looked to me as if another sister was acting selfishly and so on ... I realized I didn't love, as Jesus wanted me to love, and as he loved, difficult sisters. So I had to work hard at this, discovering numerous little ways to give myself to those who seemed at fault in one way or another. And, of course, I grew to realize that that was how God loved me too. God loved me, not because I was good but because *he* was good, merciful, forgiving. To show that my love for Jesus was a reality, it had to become visible in the love I showed for those I lived with. I discovered that when I seemed incapable of praying then *that was the very moment to give joy to Jesus through such 'nothings' as, for example, a smile, a friendly word, when I would much prefer to say nothing or look bored.*[3]

It was my experience of weakness that drew me to Jesus weak – as the holy Child and under the symbol of his suffering face. *On earth Jesus was unrecognized, hidden. I wanted the same lot to be mine. Jesus puts himself at our mercy, in a manner of speaking. He will not force us. He takes nothing unless we give it freely.*[4]

That was the secret of happiness for me – the acceptance of my humanity and the knowledge that this drew down the love of God to which I wanted to respond at every moment. Success wasn't what mattered; it was the courageous effort – even when I failed, as I so often did.

The God of Mercy

When I began my religious life I thought everything consisted in trying to be perfect through keeping lots of rules and regulations as exactly as possible. I identified holiness with good manners and a middle-class upbringing, far removed from coarse surroundings and uncongenial people. But experience and closeness to God in prayer taught me that anyone can be holy. *God doesn't call the people who are 'worthy' but the people he chooses out of love and mercy*[5] – people like myself, the weak and weepy Thérèse who had to struggle and fight with all kinds of bad tendencies, who had to face many painful truths about herself in a context where she felt herself inadequate.

God isn't looking for 'perfect' people but for people who have the guts to face the truth, to seek the truth and take its consequences; people who are willing to love God and one another in all life's messiness and pain. But don't think I'm an unhappy person. It's just the opposite. I'm always at peace because I find God everywhere, not just in 'perfect' circumstances. I've discovered that *everything* is a grace, that *everything* is matter for love. God is right here, right now.

The only science I'm interested in is the science of love, because I understand so well *that it's only love that makes us what God wants us to be and to gain it is my only ambition. Jesus has been pleased to show me the way to the divine furnace – the way of abandonment, as a little child sleeps fearlessly in its father's arms.*

75

'Let whoever is a little one come to me,' [6] *said the
Holy Spirit through the mouth of Solomon and this
same Holy Spirit has said, 'Mercy is given to little
ones.'* [7] *The prophet Isaiah reveals that on the last
day 'The Lord will lead his flock to pasture; he will
gather the young lambs and press them to his
heart.'* [8] *And as if all these promises were not
enough, the same prophet, whose inspired gaze
pierces the eternal depths, cries in the name of the
Lord; 'As a mother caresses her infant so will I
console you. You will be carried at the breasts and I
will caress you on my knees.* [9] *After reading words
like these there is nothing left but to be silent and
shed tears of gratitude and love.*

*If only all weak and imperfect souls felt as I do, I
who am the least of them all, not one would despair
of arriving at the summit of Love's mountain. Jesus
doesn't ask for great deeds but only for abandonment
and gratitude.* [10]

Remember how St Teresa loved the story of the
Samaritan woman? It's one of my favourites too.
When I think of Jesus saying to her, as he says in
the Gospel, 'Give me a drink,' [11] I realize that he is
actually asking her for love. Yet how few people
respond. *How few people give themselves to Jesus
without reserve and so are enabled to experience the
tenderness of his infinite love.* [12]

The Necessity of Great Desires

Most people think they aren't valuable enough, or
good enough to be real saints. That's a fallacy. It's
often laziness that makes them fearful of effort. I
took Joan of Arc as one of my patrons and realized I
had to be just as brave in my chosen vocation as she
was in fulfilling her own mission. I had to be ready
for suffering and face it unflinchingly even when it

76

was terribly costly and I felt weak and inadequate. *Courage doesn't consist in momentary flights of ardour which make us want to sally forth and win the world for Christ, that's just adding a touch of romance to our beautiful dreams. No, the courage that counts is the type of courage our Lord showed in the Garden of Olives. On the one hand a natural desire to turn away from suffering; on the other, the willing acceptance, even in anguish of soul, of the chalice prepared for him by the Father.*[13]

When we feel no courage or strength for the practice of virtue, then is the moment to put the axe to the root of the tree.[14] *Jesus suffered with sorrow, and here we are wanting to suffer generously, greatly!*[15] When Papa was in an asylum I thought my heart would break with sorrow. I didn't feel brave or courageous but I kept going as best I could, trusting that God would bring me through, and he did. It made me realize we can never trust God enough. I wanted to do so much for him that my desires just grew and grew. I wanted to be and to do everything at once. And yet my life was so limited, as is every life. Very few people get the opportunity to do great things and I'm no exception. I admired and envied the great saints and wondered how I could be a saint myself in my own small way.

That's when I read the Epistle of St Paul to the Corinthians where he speaks of love as the most excellent gift; it leads straight to God.[16] Then I realized that *my own vocation was to be love in the heart of the Church.*[17] Love includes everything. Love is everything. And love is available to everyone. Each of us has a capacity for love and relationships. Without love all the rest is useless.

But how could I show my love? Well, I devised a way of acting this out. During the evening silence I would go out to the great crucifix in the garden and unpetal flowers over the feet of the corpus. I do it sometimes now that I'm sick, using a crucifix laid on the bed. To me it's a symbol of complete self-giving. I let myself be despoiled for the Lord, picked to pieces like a flower. But then I have to live this symbolism out in a practical way. I try not to let any small opportunity for sacrifice slip by, no word or look to pass unnoticed. I want to suffer for love and enjoy for love; at every opportunity show God that I love him. And if I have to gather my flowers from among thorns so much the better – I shall sing even more tunefully as I go about my work.

I don't do this for myself. I make these acts of love to enrich the Church. We are all one body in Christ, everything we do affects others in a thousand hidden ways. My deeds are insignificant enough but when they are given to God he can transform them and use them to bless those who suffer, those who grieve, those who are out on the missions, those who are priests, those who are tempted ... Love is never wasted. The vocation of a Carmelite nun is to pray and to suffer for the Church, believing that prayer affects thousands who are never seen by her.

The Prayer of Surrender

You may think that with all these wonderful desires I enjoy prayer and find it a source of consolation and strength. Actually, since I first discovered I was spitting blood and was diagnosed as tubercular, heaven seems to have been shut up completely; sometimes I wonder whether I can even believe in God at all. I have the opportunity now to experience what it's like to have no faith, with all the despair that can accompany such a cast of mind. But that just means, as far as I'm concerned, that I must pray all the more, make more acts of faith, show Jesus that I love and serve him for himself, not on account of heaven.

But even before my illness, since I first entered Carmel, prayer has been very dry and arid. The only help is for me to meditate on the Gospels as I read them slowly. I try to know Jesus and put into practice all he says. I look at him in the mysteries of his life, his passion and, above all, of his suffering face. I think of the Saviour 'without beauty, without majesty'[18] and that inspires me with a love for hidden sacrifice.

I have two hours of prayer and long hours of silence during the day. I believe I have never gone three minutes without turning my thoughts towards the One I love with a cry of sorrow or gratitude. *For me, prayer means a launching out of the heart to God. It means quite simply lifting one's eyes to heaven with a cry of grateful love from the crest of joy or the trough of despair.*[19]

I'm no great soul, no eagle who rises effortlessly to the heights. *I see myself as a feeble little bird, covered only with a light down. But I have an eagle's mind and heart. In spite of my extreme littleness I dare to fix my gaze on the Divine Sun, the Sun of Love, and my heart feels all an eagle's yearnings.*[20]

So what will happen to this feeble creature who can only flap its wings and seems unable to take off? Will it die of regret at seeing itself so powerless? Not at all! *It will remain with its gaze fixed on the Divine Sun in audacious abandonment. Nothing can frighten it: neither wind nor rain nor the dark clouds which hide the Sun of Love. This little bird will not move. It knows that the sun is shining behind the clouds, its brightness never eclipsed even for a moment.*[21]

The little bird in the parable is, of course, myself. Sometimes it seems impossible to believe in anything except the dark clouds, but I keep looking towards the light even when it is invisible to all but the eyes of faith.

Neither do I lose heart when I get distracted and turn away from the Lord for a few moments. I just turn myself back again remembering that Jesus came not to call the just, but sinners, so why should I expect to be different? If God seems to be completely absent and deaf to my prayers, well, I just stay there anyway. Sometimes I even go to sleep. However, children are just as precious to their parents when they are asleep as when they are awake. Everything depends on trust and I have entrusted myself with all my weakness and sin totally to God. He can do whatever he likes with me.

I just wish I could tell everyone, all those who think they are too little or unimportant to matter to God, that they are called to holiness as much as the greatest saints. God is all merciful. If he could choose me and use me, then surely no one need despair.

The Fire of Love
When I consider how much love there is in God to be given for the asking, given for free, I desired to offer myself to receive all the love God wanted to pour out into my poor heart. I'm insignificant and frail so I didn't think of offering myself to God on behalf of other sinners for him to consume me in the fires of justice. Instead I wanted to be burnt up in the fire of love. Every heartbeat, every action, I wanted to offer to the Lord so that all the tenderness in him could be poured out into me.

Love wants to diffuse itself through being received by another. My only desire is to be like a vessel that receives the outpoured love of God and encourages others to do the same. Love breeds love, and mine is always thrusting out towards Jesus, begging for the loan of love so as to love better and to love more.

What a comfort the way of love is. You may stumble and fall on it; you may fail to measure up to grace given; but always love knows how to make the best of everything. Whatever offends our Lord is burned up in its fire and nothing is left but a deep absorbing peace.[22] I can pray:

> *Living on love is holding You Yourself,*
> *Uncreated Word, Word of my God.*
>
> *Ah! Divine Jesus, you know I love You,*
> *The Spirit of Love sets me aflame with His fire.*
> *In loving you I attract the Father,*
> *My weak heart holds him forever.*
> *O Trinity! You are a prisoner*
> *Of my love.*
>
> *Living on Love is keeping within oneself*
> *A great treasure in an earthen vase.*
> *My Beloved, my weakness is extreme,*
> *Ah! I'm far from being an angel in heaven!*
> *But if I fall with each passing hour,*
> *You come to my aid, lifting me up.*
> *At each moment You give me Your grace:*
> *I live on love.*[23]

I Choose All

Holiness is to be found in very ordinary things: in our humanity, in one another, in the Church (and in the Church nothing surprises me!). The whole meaning of the Incarnation, God becoming human, is that Jesus has entered into history and experienced our human condition unshielded. The Holy One has become one of us and can show us the way.

Most people in this community aren't aware that I've anything to say about sanctity. I don't practise great penances, I eat ordinary meals, I go to prayer when everyone else does. I don't stand out at all. But then, *holiness doesn't consist in this or that practice, but in a disposition of heart by which we rest humbly in the arms of God as little children, conscious of our weakness yet boldly confident in the goodness of our Father.*[24]

When I was four years of age an incident happened that, looking back, I see as influencing my whole life. Céline, my eight-year-old sister, and I were playing in the garden when Léonie, one of our older sisters, came along. She had a basket in which she had placed her doll and various dolls' clothes, pieces of silk, lace, velvet – the treasures of a little girl – whereas Léonie felt she was now a young lady and too old for these fancies. 'Here, darlings,' she called. 'You can have anything you want from here.' Céline looked into the basket and politely picked out a ball of coloured thread. Then it was my turn. I looked and looked … Then, after reflection, I said, 'Well, I choose everything'. And I picked up the whole basket and marched off!

That little incident was to be the mark of my whole life. *I choose everything, whatever is God's will for me. I want the whole lot!*[25] I don't just choose bits and pieces of my life, an episode here and there where I can see God's hand at work: the day of my First Communion, days of special celebration, special happiness. *I choose everything.* I choose to see God in *absolutely everything that happens,* joyful or painful, because I am his child, totally dependent on him, gratefully receiving all from him, confident that all he gives comes from the hand of One who loves me unconditionally.

But God will not force this response from us. We have to choose it and sustain it for a lifetime and that takes enormous courage and energy. God asks us to trust him with our very selves and every aspect of our lives, come what may.

True, I had a very happy home and childhood, but when I entered Carmel, my days of immaturity had to come to an end. I had to make an adult choice of Gospel childhood. I had to be an adult before I could choose childhood in a real way. This meant trusting God and continuing to trust him in every event: such as the difficulties inherent in close community living, being faithful to prayer when I didn't feel like praying, bearing the grief of Papa's long mental illness, and now my own early death creeping up, with the physical pain entailed as well as the seeming loss of faith.

I've never done great things. My life has been passed in obscurity. I've been faced only with the small daily choices everyone has to face: to be brave or cowardly, selfish or unselfish, kind or unkind. My sorrows and joys have been those of the generality. But I've tried to sustain the choice of God through them all, choosing every event as coming from the Lord, refusing him nothing, finding him every-where, wanting only to please him and return love for love. That isn't child's play, but it *is* a holiness to which *all* can aspire. Love is never wasted even when it is hidden behind walls.

Do you want God to carry you and comfort you as a mother carries and feeds her child? Do you want to know God's tenderness and care? I'm sure you do.

So why hold back? Because you are unworthy? Because you feel you're not good enough? Because you have a sinful past? Because you have failed over and over? Well, the good news is that you don't have to be worthy of God's love; you don't have to earn it. It's there waiting – pure gift, pure mercy. All you have to do is open your hands and heart to receive it with all the trust and confidence of a little child.

For Reflection

1 Thérèse had a special love for Psalm 23 (The Lord is my shepherd). Pray it with her, asking her to strengthen your faith and confidence in the love and care of God for you personally.

2 Think of some weakness or sin to which you are prone. How can you make this a stepping-stone to God?

3 The Holy Face was a focus of Thérèse's devotion because for her it symbolized Jesus' humanity, his whole person reflected in his suffering face. Find a picture of the Holy Face, such as on the shroud of Turin, and have it before you as you read the passage from Isaiah 52:13 – 53:12.

4 Thérèse said that the cheerful light of love should shine for everyone in the house without exception. Is anyone excluded from your love? If so, how can you find ways to overcome this difficulty?

5 The following prayer is taken from Thérèse's offering of herself to the merciful love of God. Read it prayerfully and make it your own as far as you can.

In order that my life may be one act of perfect love
I offer myself as a whole burnt offering to your merciful love,
begging you to consume me without ceasing.
May the waves of infinite tenderness contained within you overflow into my soul
so that I may become a martyr of your love, O Lord.

NOTES
1 *The Story of Soul*, chapter 2
2 *Ibid*, chapter 9
3 Letter 122, *Collected Letters of St Thérèse*, trans. F. Sheed, Sheed and Ward, 1949
4 Letter 123, ibid
5 *The Story of a Soul*, chapter 1
6 Proverbs 9:4
7 Wisdom 6:7
8 Isaiah 40:11
9 Isaiah 66:12–13
10 Manuscript B
11 John 4:7
12 Manuscript B
13 Witness of Sr Genevieve (Thérèse's sister Céline), *A Memoir of My Sister St Thérèse*, Sr Genevieve, trans. Carmelite Sisters of New York, M. H. Gill & Son, 1959, p. 191
14 Letter 40, *Collected Letters of St Thérèse*, op. cit
15 Letter 55, ibid
16 1 Corinthians 13
17 Manuscript B
18 Isaiah 53:2
19 *The Story of a Soul*, chapter 37
20 Manuscript B
21 *Ibid*
22 *The Story of a Soul*, chapter 29
23 Poem 17, vv. 2, 7, *The Poetry of St Thérèse of Lisieux*, trans. D. Kinney ODC, ICS Publications, 1996
24 *Last Conversations*
25 *The Story of a Soul*, chapter 1

Chapter 6

God Dwells Within –
Elizabeth of the Trinity

Blessed Elizabeth of the Trinity (1880–1906) was a
near-contemporary of St Thérèse, but of a very
different temperament. Born Elizabeth Catez in the
military barracks at Bourges, her father, from a
very poor peasant family, had risen through the
ranks to become an officer. The strength of his
ambition can be gauged by the fact that he waited to
marry until he received his commission, only then,
in his forties, did he wed an officer's daughter four-
teen years his junior. He obviously did not intend
that his hard-won position should be compromised
by marriage to a woman of a lower class who could
not complement her husband in his rising career.

Elizabeth's early years were spent in a military
environment and it is noteworthy that all her
family visits and connections seem to have been
with her mother's relatives and not with her
father's. Two and a half years after Elizabeth's birth

she was joined by another sister, Marguerite (Guite). Captain Catez died when Elizabeth was seven and Madame Catez, Elizabeth (Sabeth as she was called in her family circle) and Guite moved into an apartment in Dijon where they lived in relative comfort and were to become an inseparable trio.

Elizabeth never attended school. She showed considerable musical talent and spent many hours daily at the piano. She studied at the Dijon Conservatory and had private instruction in general subjects at home. Her education remained incomplete but was considered perfectly adequate for a young girl of her time.

Sabeth and Guite lived full social lives, travelling with their mother, attending parties, dances and musical soirées. Both dressed with taste and elegance and took part in the entertainments and diversions of other young people.

But there was another side to Elizabeth's character that gradually attained dominance. She was by temperament strong-willed and choleric – her father's daughter. By degrees she brought this under control so as to avoid hurting her mother. Her First Confession, First Communion and Confirmation were all milestones in her growing attraction to a life lived within.

In deference to Madame Catez's wishes, Elizabeth deferred her entry into Carmel until she was twenty-one. A year later Guite married George Chevignard, a banker. She would bear him nine children. Sabeth and Odile, the first two, were born while Elizabeth was still alive, and she took a lively interest in them and in all Guite's affairs.

In the Carmel of Dijon, Elizabeth surrendered herself completely to the interior prayer which drew her so strongly, but she never forgot that what she herself was living within the enclosure was the heritage of all baptized Christians, each one a temple of the Holy Spirit. Also, Elizabeth had learned how to live this truth even in the midst of her social engagements as a laywoman, and was eager to communicate her 'secret' to her friends and family in her letters and conversations.

Elizabeth died of Addison's disease at the age of twenty-six.

She speaks to us from the other side of the grille in the convent parlour. The most noticeable physical feature of this young woman is her eyes – large and very dark with dark brows. She conveys an impression of deep stillness.

Elizabeth Speaks

I was a terrible child, while my sister was all gentleness and pliability. You could hardly imagine the tantrums and scenes I used to make if I couldn't get my own way – and *right* away! Yet underneath I already had a strong attraction to prayer and, as in all things, if I wanted anything I made sure I got it. The struggle with my bad tendencies was unrelenting but it was made easier because of the love I had for my mother and sister. I would do anything to avoid hurting them; I loved them so much. We were everything to one another after my father's death.

When I was eight I began studying music at the Dijon Conservatory. I knew I had a lot of talent in that direction. Everything in me vibrates with music. It fills my being and, when I was young, was an outlet for my enormous creative energy that needed some direction. But I was also drawn powerfully to silence. It seems to me that at the heart of all truly great music there is a silence where what cannot be communicated comes into its own. One of the most difficult renunciations I have had to make in coming to Carmel is the renunciation of music – playing, and listening to classical composers – my music is all now in the silence of the Trinity, a music that cannot be heard but which still vibrates inside me.

By the time I was sixteen my music instructors were forecasting a future for me as a concert performer; I was much in demand as a pianist and sight read excellently; it made me a welcome guest wherever I went. Because of my enormous energy and directedness I could never understand how anyone could live in a half-hearted manner. I resolved early on that God would be the Love of my life and it was for him that I struggled so hard with my rage and fits of temper. I didn't want to be the slave of a capricious 'artistic temperament'.

I received an intimation of my future vocation as a Carmelite when, on the day of my First Communion, I was taken to visit the Prioress at the nearby Carmel. As a souvenir she gave me a holy card, telling me that my name meant 'house of God'. That opened up a new world. God was within my heart, not only at Holy Communion but always. The Trinity was dwelling within me. Since then I've found great significance in names and was delighted when I heard that in Carmel my name would be Marie-Elizabeth of the Trinity. *It is there, in the depths of my soul, in my interior heaven, that I love to find the Lord, since he never leaves me. I think my name indicates a special vocation; I so love the mystery of the Trinity, it is an abyss in which I lose myself.*[1]

It was the drawing to God within that helped me to focus myself while living a very full social life. We loved to travel as a family and I was moved by the beauties of nature. Yet all the time my heart was being drawn back to God even while I enjoyed everything to the full. For example, on holiday at St Hilaire *they gave us such fine feasts that our stomachs were begging for mercy*.[2] Then at Limoux my friend had an excellent baby grand which was my delight. It had a superb tone. I could spend hours at it playing four-hand music by sight with another friend's husband.

Even though my longing was for solitude in order to develop the growing attraction I felt for prayer, I didn't make the mistake of thinking I could only find God when I was in a more conducive environment. I was the 'house of God' whether helping in the parish, relaxing at home, practising the piano, dancing ... You name it – God was there, living within me and I with him.

When I came to Carmel at the age of twenty-one, I was already a person attuned to inner silence and this has been the great attraction which I want others to benefit from. My sister Guite is married and I don't think for a moment that she is called to lesser union with God. When I was reading in St Paul about the mystery of divine adoption I naturally thought of her for, as a mother, she would understand from experience the depths of love there is in a maternal heart for one's children. Even in the midst of her domestic cares she can live in the centre of her soul, surrendering to the Holy Spirit, being transformed into the likeness of Christ.[3]

Teacher of Prayer
My special grace seems to be to bear witness to a

life with the God who is all Love and who is encountered in the depths of the heart of the baptized person. This life grows gradually through getting to know and to love Christ, accepting the intimacy he offers. If you too got to know Christ even a little you would come to him with the greatest simplicity, heart to heart, whether you felt devotional or not.

I didn't have to wait to be clothed in the Carmelite habit before endeavouring to make my life one continuing prayer and encouraging my friends along the same lines. Naturally this prayer cannot be explicit all the time, but a life which unites faith and love finds Christ in every occupation. *The good God is to be found just as much at the washing up as at prayer time.*[4]

So much hinges upon a recollection which fosters the inner silence I recommend to all. It's far more a question of *interior silence* although an outward silence helps if you can get it. *Recollection means entering into one's own depths, from which we are often absent, so that although God comes with his gifts he finds no one; the soul is outside, caught up in exterior things instead of dwelling within itself, in the depths.*[5] We live so much on the periphery of life, it's all too easy to lose this sense of being more than we appear on the surface.

Prayer is to find the Master deep down in one's own soul.[6] It is independent of exterior occupations and has everything to do with maintaining an inner freedom, not being swept away by passing fancies. *It seems to me that nothing can distract from God when you act for none but him, continually in his holy presence. God's gaze penetrates the most intimate regions of the soul, so that even in the midst of the world you can listen to him in the silence of*

92

your heart when it wants to exist only for him.[7] To recollect oneself is to keep one's strength for the Lord.

Adoration

For me, adoration means the continual forgetting of self so as to attend to the Divine at each moment. *A soul which is preoccupied with self, which indulges in useless thoughts and desires scatters its forces; it is not completely under God's sway. Its lyre is not in tune, so that when the Master strikes it he cannot draw forth divine harmonies. It is too human and discordant.*[8] I want to be a continual 'Praise of Glory', always in tune with God, and that demands simplicity and self-forgetfulness. Self-forgetfulness doesn't have to be specifically God-remembering; it can be the self-forgetfulness that is demanded of Guite when she has to care for her children. What matters is not putting self and one's own sensibilities at the forefront of consciousness all the time, as we tend to do.

I believe that my mission will be to draw souls by helping them to go out of themselves.[9] Only the love of Christ gives the necessary motivation and strength for this. And don't forget, I had to struggle long and hard with my own temperament to become simple and directed. There is a real death involved in leaving self-preoccupation. *We have to say with St Paul 'I die daily', otherwise you can be hidden at certain times in God but you don't live habitually with the Divine Being because all your feelings, personal interests and so forth drag you away.*[10]

Adoration is a word that fascinates me, it seems to come straight from heaven. Adoration is to gaze upon God in deepest silence, in profound peace. It is to live by faith. Sometimes it is very hard to remain

93

before God when I feel nothing but darkness and pain. *Then is the time to awaken my faith and to prefer not to find joy in his presence in order that he might find joy in my love.*[11] Friendship with God, who is closer to us than we are to ourselves, is not a matter of feeling and imagination, *it's a matter of pure faith.*[12] Prayer can be described as a watching in faith, attentive in love to the holy reality of God's unbounded presence. That's a reality for each one of us, and leads to transformation in Christ, the goal of our lives as Christians, whoever we are and wherever we may be.

Adoration is consummated in union, in love, and it begins here on earth. *A soul united to Jesus is a living smile which radiates him and gives him.*[13] *Indeed I have found heaven on earth because heaven is God and God is in my soul. The day I understood this everything became clear to me. I wish to tell this secret very softly to those whom I love so that they, through everything, may always cling to God.*[14]

Janua Coeli

Janua coeli is a name I've given to the little statue I have of our Lady of Lourdes. I've been to Lourdes and it is a place of unsurpassed prayer. *Janua coeli* is Latin for 'gate of heaven'. As a Carmelite, Mary introduces me to the life of adoration and conse-crated love – heaven on earth.

When I contemplate Mary I see her as the silent one for whom the most important things take place within. *The Virgin's attitude during the months which passed between the Annunciation and the Nativity is the model for interior souls. In what peace and recollection did Mary live and act? Yet that did not prevent her from spending herself for others when charity required. The Gospel tells us*

that Mary, rising up, went in haste into the hill
country to a city of Judah to visit her cousin Eliza-
beth. Never did the ineffable vision she contemplated
within her make her lessen her charity to others.[15]

The Virgin of the Incarnation is the one who pre-
eminently kept all things in her heart. As she
formed Christ within her womb, so I pray that she
may form me too in his image, the image of her
Firstborn, the Son of God. My whole vocation is
Marian: to be virgin and mother as Mary was.
Virgin – espoused to Christ in faith; 'mother' –
saving souls and multiplying the adopted children
of the Father. Prayer can never be for oneself alone.

In every life there will be elements of suffering
and sacrifice. Choices can be hard to make, there is
death and despoliation in a thousand ways, great
and small. Mary too was pierced secretly within her
heart. *It is there, in the depths of my own heart, that*
I meet suffering and still find peace, waiting beneath
the cross with Jesus' mother, hearing him say to me
as to John 'Behold your mother'.[16] *Mary still stands*
with me beneath my own cross on which 'I fill up the
things that are wanting in the sufferings of Christ
for the sake of his body, the Church'.[17] *Mary is there*
to teach me to suffer as he did, enabling me to hear
the last outpourings of Christ's soul which only a
mother could catch.[18]

Mary was the 'house of God' in a unique way as
Godbearer. No one can reveal to me the secret of
total surrender as she can, as I wrote in a poem I
composed at Christmas time.

> 'House of God', I have within me the prayer
> Of Jesus Christ, the divine adorer,
> It takes me to souls and to the Father,
> As that is its double movement.

To be saviour with my Master,
That is also my mission.
So I must disappear,
Lose myself in Him through union.
 Jesus, Word of life,
 United to You forever,
 Your virgin and Your victim
 Will radiate Your love:
 'Amo Christum.'

Mother of the Word, oh tell me your mystery.
After the moment of the Incarnation,
Tell me how you spent your life
Buried in adoration.
 In a peace wholly ineffable,
 A mysterious silence,
 You entered the Unfathomable Being,
 Bearing within you 'the gift of God'.
  Oh, keep me always
  In the divine embrace.
  May I bear the imprint
  Of this God of all Love:
  'Amo Christum.' [19]

25 December 1903

The Dynamics of Prayer[20]

Everyone could doubtless object that there are
numerous ways for an enclosed nun to be reminded
of God's presence, but it is much more difficult for
busy people who have jobs, families, careers and
a thousand distractions. There is so little time
available, one is tired by evening, one does not know
how to pray ...

The only advice I can give is: begin anyway. You
learn to pray by praying. If you do not get into the
water, the best advice on swimming is useless. If

you do not know how to pray just tell the Lord, ask for help. Find moments when there is a break and use them: waiting for a bus, at a red light, while standing in line at the supermarket checkout. *I used to find travelling by train an ideal opportunity.*[21] Wherever you are find brief moments to recall God's presence. Pray for those with whom you are working, those who come to mind as you fetch and carry, those who travel on the same transport ... There are so many ways to catch a moment in which to adore, to thank, to praise, to intercede.

I used to send an arrow of prayer to the Lord when I was at parties and dances during the holidays. Finally, Jesus became the Friend of my every moment, *a beloved Person from whom one can no longer be separated.*[22]

It is a matter of educating oneself, applying oneself, getting used to living always beneath the eye of God and in his company. I know that I will not live much longer, that there will be a lot of pain to endure from the disease that has begun to consume my body, but I always try to get beneath the surface and find the Lord in order to make him the gift of myself. It is a gift to others too if you can remain outwardly happy. *In the beginning, as I know well, you have to make efforts when you feel boiling inside, but quite gently, by means of patience and with the good Lord, you eventually succeed.*[23]

Even sins and miseries can add grist to the mill. It's not so much a question of loving as letting yourself be loved. Letting go of all else and allowing God to work in you all he wants. *Let yourself be loved.*[24] Wait, watch, surrender, adore. *It is so simple. Take the crucifix, look, listen.*[25]

Prayer to the Trinity

On 21 November, after renewing my vows with the community on the feast of the Presentation of Mary in the temple, I composed a prayer that I consider a true reflection of my soul, of all that I want to say and to share. The attitude of inner peace and stillness is a mark of my approach. God is so great. He is an abyss in which I want to lose myself. He is the focus of my love and my life: Father, Son and Holy Spirit.

> O my God
> Trinity whom I adore,
> help me to forget myself entirely
> that I may be established in You
> as still and as peaceful
> as if my soul were already in eternity.
> May nothing trouble my peace
> or make me leave You,
> O my Unchanging One,
> but may each minute
> carry me further
> into the depths of Your Mystery.
> Give peace to my soul;
> make it Your heaven,
> Your beloved dwelling
> and Your resting place.
> May I never leave You there alone
> but be wholly present,
> my faith wholly vigilant,
> wholly adoring,
> and wholly surrendered
> to Your creative Action.
>
> O my beloved Christ,
> crucified by love,
> I wish to be a bride

for Your Heart;
I wish to cover You with glory;
I wish to love You …
even to dying of it!
But I feel my weakness,
and I ask You
to 'clothe me with Yourself',
to identify my soul
with all the movements of Your Soul,
to overwhelm me,
to possess me,
to substitute Yourself for me
that my life may be
but a radiance of Your Life.
Come into me as Adorer,
as Restorer,
as Saviour.

O Eternal Word,
Word of my God,
I want to spend my life
in listening to You,
to become wholly teachable
that I may learn all from You.
Then, through all nights,
all voids,
all helplessness,
I want to gaze on You always
and remain in Your great light.
O my beloved Star,
so fascinate me
that I may not withdraw
from Your radiance.

O consuming Fire,
Spirit of Love,
'come upon me',

and create in my soul
a kind of incarnation of the Word:
that I may be
another humanity for Him
in which He can renew His whole Mystery.
And You, O Father,
bend lovingly
over Your poor little creature;
'cover her with Your shadow',
seeing in her
only the 'Beloved
in whom You are well pleased'.

O my Three,
my All,
my Beatitude,
infinite Solitude,
Immensity in which I lose myself,
I surrender myself to You
as Your prey.
Bury Yourself in me
that I may bury myself in You
until I depart to contemplate
in Your light
the abyss of Your greatness.

21 November 1904

I'm still the same Elizabeth who was such a
passionate child, so musical, so friendly, so
engaging in company. But I have mastered my
excessive sensitivity and brought the music of my
life into harmony with the divine music of heaven,
at the heart of which is a silence that draws me *to
life, to love, to light.*[26]

For Reflection

1 Pray Elizabeth's 'Prayer to the Trinity' slowly. What does this prayer say to you in your own search for God?

2 'Take the crucifix, look, listen,' Elizabeth wrote to Guite. Light a candle before a representation of Christ Crucified and gaze silently in adoration and praise.

3 Silence was a great attraction in Elizabeth's life. Are there ways in which you can find more space for silence in a busy day, even if only for a few minutes?

4 Consider your Christian name and find out its meaning. Is there in it some special intimation of your personal vocation such as Elizabeth found in hers?

5 'The Blessed Trinity is our dwelling place, our home, our Father's house, which we should never leave.' Do these words resonate with you? Elizabeth wrote them to her sister, a wife and mother. She obviously thought they were meant for everyone, not just those whose lives are more withdrawn from society. How can you foster this interior life in your own way? Compose a prayer to verbalize your aspirations.

NOTES
All quotations are taken from *Elizabeth of the Trinity – The Complete Works*, trans. Sr Aletheia Kane ODC, ICS Publications, 1984.

1 Letter 62
2 Letter 11
3 cf Letter 239
4 Letter 89
5 Letter 302
6 Letter 161
7 Letter 38

8 Last Retreat
9 Letter 335
10 Last Retreat
11 Letter 289
12 Letter 236
13 Letter 252
14 Letter 122
15 Heaven on Earth Prayer 12
16 John 19:27
17 Col. 1:24
18 Last Retreat
19 Poem 88
20 This section owes much to the work of Conrad de Meester ODC
21 cf Letter 287
22 Letter 280
23 Letter 123
24 Testimony left to Mother Genevieve
25 Letter 88
26 Elizabeth's last words

Epilogue

And what of myself, the author of these pages? Can I find myself in this book – my own prayer, my own search for integrity and inner peace? Yes and no. Yes, because these men and women are my sisters and brothers in the Order; we share a common history, a common life style according to a Rule which blends solitude and community. Our life-experience has many meeting points. These people are my friends and mentors. And no – because I am a woman of a different time and culture. The concerns of today are not those of yesterday: the concerns of collegiality, the empowerment of women, the option for the poor, ecology, justice and peace ... And as a woman of today's world I am interested in areas of life that did not touch my predecessors in the Order, who had different interests in a different social milieu.

But Carmelite spirituality is deeper and wider than any one person or group. It penetrates to the deepest roots of our being where each one meets God as a unique person. It is a spirituality of relationships – with God and others in the fulness of our humanity. The more truly human we are the more we shall meet others and share what is deepest, what makes us one. It is at this level, where each relates to God, that the saints of Carmel will be perennially relevant.

The prophetic aspect of the Order, mirrored in Elijah, impels the Carmelite towards a radically counter-cultural life style that will, in varying degrees, embody the prophet's silence on Horeb and his challenge to the people of Israel to love

103

justice. The prayerful element, embodied in Mary, is that of total surrender to the Lord in a covenant of self-giving love which bears Christ for the world. Carmel is pre-eminently Marian and as a Marian Order, finds in her its fullest expression.

As I write this, we are about to celebrate Christmas which I always consider the greatest feast of the Mendicants. We shall be singing round the Crib, we shall be talking and laughing together as we eat piles of toast and marmalade at one of our few 'talking breakfasts' of the year; we will be silently pondering on the mystery of the Incarnation, holding the world in our hearts during the hours of prayer. We will celebrate the liturgy with a new wonder at God's tender mercy, and we will be on the threshold of another year as we commemorate Mary's motherhood and all that flows from it.

Carmelite spirituality is deeply human and humane because this is what prayer accomplishes in us. Carmelite spirituality understands and accepts weakness. It makes allowances for difference. It challenges and supports the seeker after God. It does not give answers to problems but allows them to be held in prayer so that action ultimately springs from the centre of a person's being and is not an unfocussed activism.

The land of Carmel affirms God's continual presence while allowing us to experience human pain and the anguish of the world. In God's presence and before his face we shall ask the right questions and realize ultimately that God is *all*. In God we have everything, including, and indeed most especially, our deepest humanity, for he is Emmanuel: God-with-us.

The alternative prayer for the Second Sunday after Christmas seems to put everything much better than I can:

Father of our Lord Jesus Christ,
our glory is to stand before the world
as your own sons and daughters.
May the simple beauty of Jesus' birth
summon us always to love what is most deeply
human,
and to see your Word made flesh
reflected in those whose lives we touch.

Suggestions for Further Reading

Carmelite Spirituality (General)
Slattery P., *The Springs of Carmel*, St Paul, 1990
Valebek R., *Prayer Life in Carmel*, Carmel in the World Paperbacks, 1982

St Teresa of Avila
Bilecki T., *Teresa of Avila, Mystical Writings*, Burns and Oates, 1994
Obbard E. R., *La Madre*, St Paul, 1994
Teresa of Avila *Collected Works*. There are several good translations available.
Williams R., *Teresa of Avila*, G. Chapman, 1991

St John of the Cross
Burrows R., *Ascent to Love, The Teaching of St John of the Cross*, DLT, 1987
Hardy R., *The Life of St John of the Cross*, DLT, 1987
John of the Cross *Complete Works*. There are several good translations available.
Matthew I. *The Impact of God*, DLT, 1996

Brother Lawrence
Lawrence Bro. *The Practice of the Presence of God*, trans. D. Attwater, Burns and Oates, 1977

St Thérèse of Lisieux
Gaucher G., *The Spiritual Journey of St Thérèse of Lisieux*, DLT, 1987
Hollings M. *Thérèse of Lisieux*, Fount, 1982

Meester C. de, *With Empty Hands*, Burns and Oates, 1987

Thérèse of Lisieux *The Story of a Soul*, trans. John Clarke, ICS Publications, 1975

Elizabeth of the Trinity

Elizabeth of the Trinity *Light Love Life*, ed. C. de Meester, ICS Publications, 1984

Von Balthasar H.U. *Two Sisters in the Spirit* (Thérèse and Elizabeth), Ignatius Press, 1992